*Join the Revolution*

# SPIRITUAL A.I
## The Authentic Intelligence
Awareness and Intuition: Your Inner Technology

By Leonie Du Toit

Copyright © 2025 by Leonie Du Toit

All rights reserved.

No part of this publication may be reproduced, stored in a retrieval system, or transmitted in any form or by any means—electronic, mechanical, photocopying, recording, scanning, or otherwise—without the prior written permission of the author, except in the case of brief quotations used in reviews, articles, or other non-commercial uses permitted by copyright law.

This book is based on the author's personal experiences, client stories (shared with permission or anonymously), and spiritual teachings. It is intended for informational and inspirational purposes only and is not intended to diagnose, treat, cure, or prevent any medical or psychological condition. The contents of this book do not constitute medical advice, mental health advice, or professional therapy. Always consult a qualified healthcare professional for any questions or concerns regarding your physical or mental health.

The Traffic Light Game is an original tool created by Leonie Du Toit. It may be used for personal practice and shared non-commercially with proper credit. However, it may not be used in paid programs, coaching materials, or teaching environments without the express written permission of the author. All rights to the name and method remain with the creator.

The A.I. Code, along with other insights shared in this book, may be used freely for personal exploration and reflection. The author disclaims any liability for outcomes resulting from the application of any material contained herein.

First Edition

ISBN: 978-0-646-72395-2

For more information, visit: www.leoniedutoit.com

THIS MOMENT RIGHT HERE

IS WHERE YOU OPEN A DOOR

TO THE MOST POWERFUL

PART OF YOURSELF.

# DEDICATION

I want to dedicate this book to my two beautiful daughters, Febe and Chloe. I trust and believe that the little things I taught you about awareness and intuition will always guide you for your highest good. I love you.

Then I would like to acknowledge my higher self, my awareness. I am so grateful to have such a strong connection with my inner voice and will continue to honour it and follow with trust.

I also want to dedicate this book to all the beautiful souls who have been drawn to it. This book found you for a reason, and I know that everything in it can help you use your inner intelligence and step into a life of clarity, ease, and purpose.

I know that when you step into a life of awareness, you will live a full and happy life, always guided, moment to moment, by the voice of your soul.

## FOREWORD

As I read Leonie's book, I felt an immediate recognition—like a message I too carry was being spoken aloud. In her words lives a revolution, not of rebellion, but of reconnection. A return to the intelligence we each hold within: our awareness, our intuition, our truth.

This book isn't just information—it's a transmission. It calls us to remember what we've always known deep down: that the answers we seek aren't out there. They're in us.

Leonie's clarity, honesty, and devotion to self-awareness ripple outward. Her work is a gift for this time—a steady light for those ready to live from the inside out.

I'm grateful to walk beside her in this movement. Together, we are anchoring a new way—one rooted in presence, self-trust, and truth.

May this book awaken what has always lived in you.

Daniella Princi
Holistic and Spiritual Psychologist, Intuitive & Energy Worker.
www.daniellaprinci.com

## CONTENTS

| | |
|---|---|
| Introduction | Pg 1 |
| Chapter 1:  Starting a Revolution | Pg 7 |
| Chapter 2:  Awareness - The Key to Everything | Pg 17 |
| Chapter 3:  The How-to of Building Awareness | Pg 43 |
| Chapter 4:  Intuition – The Voice of the Soul | Pg 70 |
| Chapter 5:  Intuition – The Practice of Listening | Pg 91 |
| Chapter 6:  Awareness in Self and Spiritual-Development | Pg 109 |
| Chapter 7:  Awareness in Healing | Pg 147 |
| Chapter 8:  Awareness in Relationship | Pg 175 |
| Chapter 9:  Awareness with and in our children | Pg 226 |
| Chapter 10:  Awakening Abundance | Pg 243 |
| Chapter 11:  Awareness in Everyday Life | Pg 274 |
| Chapter 12:  The A.I. Code in the Growth Industry | Pg 287 |
| Chapter 13:  The Revolution | Pg 296 |
| Chapter 14:  The Spiritual A.I. Toolkit | Pg 299 |
| Chapter 15:  Bonus – 30 Day Journal | Pg 331 |
| Note from the Author | Pg 363 |
| About the Author | Pg 364 |

SPIRITUAL A.I.

# INTRODUCTION

Life has become confusing, chaotic, and overwhelming. Our attention has been pulled away from our inner world, where our true strength and power reside, and scattered across the noise of the outer world. We are bombarded with distractions that captivate our body, mind, and spirit, drawing us further from ourselves. We have handed over our power to those who claim to know what's best for us, blindly following authority without question.

In this disconnect, we have become slaves to technology and those manipulating it to influence us. Addicted to the fleeting dopamine rush, we seek temporary relief from an emptiness we don't fully understand. Like hollow vessels, we drift through life searching for something, anything to fill the void and make us feel whole again. We long for clarity, ease, and purpose, yet we have no idea how to attain them. So, we keep looking outside ourselves, hoping that more money, fame, love, or possessions will finally bring the fulfilment we crave. Still, this endless external search only keeps us trapped on the hamster wheel, running in place yet going nowhere.

Most people feel profoundly disconnected. They move through their days on autopilot, caught in cycles of stress, struggle, and stagnation, unaware that the answers they seek have been within them all along. If they stopped chasing and became still, they would find everything they ever wanted and needed to feel whole.

So why do so many people feel lost? Why do we continue searching outside ourselves? Because society has conditioned us to believe that the answers lie elsewhere. We are told that intuition is "just our imagination," that creativity is a waste of time, and that there is something wrong with us if we can't sit still in a classroom. If we don't fit the system's mould, we are labelled as failures, told we are stupid, not good enough, broken, and destined to fall short. We are placed in a box, given a label, and pressured to conform. I know firsthand what it's like to be broken down and humiliated for not fitting into that box.

School was a struggle for me, especially math. Not because I wasn't capable, but because I needed more time to figure things out. But instead of support, I was met with ridicule. My primary school math teacher decided that the best way to handle my incomplete homework was to put me into a rubbish bin, an act that created a massive block in my learning and self-worth.

Then there was the time I gave an honest answer in class, only to be laughed at by the teacher and her students, the teachers' pets, making me feel stupid and small. Or the time I was asked to read in front of the class, and instead of encouragement, I was met with harsh criticism, reinforcing the belief that I wasn't good enough. I didn't fit in, and they made sure I knew it.

I carried those wounds for years, believing that my differences were flaws. But over time, I began to see the truth, the very things they tried to break in me are now my greatest strengths.

I am no longer in that box. I was never meant to be in it.

They say that our struggles shape our purpose, that the things that once held us back become the lessons we are meant to teach. For me, every challenge, every moment of being told I wasn't enough, only fuelled my journey to reclaim my power.

But true power isn't found in rebellion against the system; it's found in reconnecting with what was never lost: our inner intelligence, awareness, and intuition. The world teaches us to conform and seek answers outside ourselves, but the truth is, everything we need has always been within.

This book is my offering to the world, a guide to reclaiming your inner power by mastering the dance between awareness and intuition. It is an invitation to step into a new way of being, one where you are fully present, deeply connected, and able to create a life of clarity, ease, and purpose.

## Why Spiritual AI?

Technology is advancing faster than ever, yet as we become more connected to machines, we become less connected to ourselves. The human race is being removed from itself, distracted by screens, algorithms, and artificial intelligence. We are drowning in information but starving for wisdom. But there is another kind of AI: Awareness and Intuition.

This is the intelligence we must reclaim. When we develop our inner "technology", our ability to be profoundly aware and intuitively guided, we unlock a power greater than anything artificial intelligence could ever provide. Tapping into these two spiritual senses is the greatest act of self-love that we can commit to. It is how we will see what's wrong and right in this world and what is right for us and our path. This is how we change the world. Let's start a revolution.

## My Journey with Awareness & Intuition

From a young age, I was fascinated by people, their body language, the words they didn't say, the patterns they couldn't see in themselves. When I first started working, right out of school, I would sit outside the shop on the edge of a water fountain during my lunch break and watch the people walk past, picking up on their energy, facial expressions, and emotions. This led me to self-study a bit of body language, words (statement analysis) and what they reveal. I did a lot of self-development and dove into spirituality, but the real transformation came through awareness. I will share how my journey with awareness started in a later chapter.

Growing up in a home with an alcoholic father*, I learned the power of observation. I became hyper-aware of my surroundings, picking up on subtle shifts in energy, tone, and emotions. What started as a survival mechanism evolved into my greatest gift, the ability to see what others miss. A heightened sense of awareness. My fascination with people and their behaviours and habits grew stronger and stronger. By the time I reached my final year at school, I knew I wanted to work with people and help them. I wanted to study Psychology. The thing is, my grades were not "good enough" for me to go to university. I wasn't even "good enough" to go to college to become a teacher either. The system didn't support me; I was told I wasn't good enough.

Even though my grades were too bad to get me into university to study psychology or become a teacher, I still managed to follow my soul to where I am today, helping people transform their lives.

*Note: I'm very grateful that my dad found Christ by the time I went to high school. I love my mom and dad very much.

Learning what makes people tick and what's under the surface, like the words they use and the energy they carry, is still my passion, and with my unique skills, I can help people create a life of clarity, ease and purpose.

Today, I believe that one conversation with me in a coaching session could change everything. In fact, I own this with gratitude and humility; it has changed hundreds of my clients' lives.

I realised that awareness wasn't just about observing others but understanding myself. I began to notice my own thoughts, patterns, and behaviours, and in doing so, I unlocked something profound: the ability to change.

As I deepened my awareness, I also started trusting my intuition. I learned that my gut feelings were seldom wrong; only my mind doubted them. I began to listen, follow the nudges, and step into a life that felt guided rather than forced. Now, I help others do the same.

Throughout this book, you will learn how to cultivate awareness, trust your intuition, and awaken your inner intelligence. You will discover how to break free from limiting beliefs, patterns, and conditioning. You will learn to navigate life with clarity, ease, and purpose. Are you ready to unlock the real AI within you?

# CHAPTER 1

# STARTING A SPIRITUAL REVOLUTION

Artificial Intelligence (AI) is designed to analyse, calculate, and optimise. It can process massive amounts of data, predict patterns, and automate decisions with precision. But AI lacks something fundamental: consciousness. It does not feel, perceive, or intuit. It operates purely on logic, disconnected from the deeper wisdom that guides the human experience.

Spiritual AI, which is Awareness and Intuition, operates differently. It is not based on external data but on inner clarity. It doesn't rely on algorithms. It relies on presence and deep knowing. It is the intelligence that moves through us, guiding us toward alignment, purpose, and truth.

Where AI mimics intelligence, Spiritual AI is intelligence.

The real revolution is not in developing smarter machines. It is in reclaiming our ability to be profoundly aware and intuitively guided. And when enough people awaken to this, everything changes. They say if you want to change the world, start with yourself. This is how: by becoming aware, by healing what hurts, and by growing into who you truly are. From there, the change ripples outward, first to our partners, then to our children, and eventually to the world. True transformation begins within. Its impact is limitless.

**How Will This Change the World?**

> *"Awareness is the greatest agent for change.",*
> *-Eckhart Tolle*

The world is at a turning point. We are more connected than ever through technology, yet more disconnected from ourselves and each other. We are drowning in information but starving for wisdom. We chase external validation, mistaking it for fulfilment, and wonder why we still feel lost.

The solution to this chaos isn't more knowledge, more strategies, or more control. It's not about fixing what's wrong out there. The answer lies within us. Awareness and intuition are the two most powerful tools we have for transforming not only our own lives but the world itself.

Awareness is what allows us to see clearly. It's like someone turning the lights on in a room you didn't even realise was dark. Suddenly, you notice the dust, the clutter, the things that don't belong. But you also see the beauty that was always there, hidden underneath it all. Awareness brings truth into view. It helps you understand that what you've been carrying was never really yours. It dissolves the illusion of separation and awakens the wholeness that's always lived inside you.

When we cultivate awareness, we begin to see beyond the illusions that keep us trapped. We recognise the patterns, conditioning, and fears that have shaped our decisions. Awareness is the light that reveals truth. The truth about who we are, what we desire, and what no longer serves us. With awareness, we step out of autopilot and reclaim our power to consciously create our lives. And when we trust our intuition, we align with a deeper intelligence. One that is beyond logic but never without wisdom. Intuition is our direct connection to the divine collective. It guides us toward expansion, possibility, and purpose. It is the voice that whispers when something is off before we have proof. It is the nudge that says, go this way, when reason says otherwise. When we listen to our intuition, we navigate life with ease, making decisions that feel right at the deepest level.

Imagine a world where people are fully aware of their own power. Where instead of blindly following systems designed to keep them small, they trust themselves. Where instead of being ruled by fear, they are led by an inner knowing. A world where we no longer look to external authorities for permission but instead turn inward for answers. A world where people no longer feel lost, stuck, or unworthy, because they remember who they are.

This is not some distant fantasy. It is a reality waiting to be awakened. And it begins with you. By reclaiming your awareness and intuition, you are not just changing your own life. You are shifting the collective consciousness. You are becoming part of the awakening that will transform the world. And it all starts here.

**Where My Journey with Awareness Started**

> *"Until you make the unconscious conscious, it will direct your life, and you will call it fate."*
>
> *- Carl Jung*

I was in my early twenties, living in Johannesburg, South Africa, trying to build a life I thought was right. I had moved in with my then boyfriend and was working for his family, helping run their small café. From the outside, it may have looked like I was settling into adulthood, doing what people expected—living with a partner, holding a job, and playing the part. But inside, I was slowly unravelling.

The family dynamics were heavy with unspoken truths and tangled loyalties. Every day felt like walking on eggshells. I didn't feel seen, safe, or like myself. The pressure kept mounting until one day, something inside me just cracked. I wasn't proud of who I had become, either. I felt lost, disconnected from myself and from any sense of meaning or joy. I couldn't see a way out.

Then came the afternoon that changed everything.

I was alone in the apartment. The silence around me was deafening, matching the numbness I felt inside. In a moment of deep despair, I sat down, wrote a note, swallowed a handful of sleeping pills, and lay down on the bed. I was done. I just wanted the pain to stop.

But life had other plans.

I woke up to my boyfriend shaking me violently, his voice panicked, dragging me down the stairs and into the car. The next thing I remember was the cold brightness of the hospital lights and the burn of shame and confusion as they pumped my stomach. I stayed overnight. No one really knew what to say. There were no soft landings, no warm arms waiting. I had no family nearby. No therapist. No real support systems. I had to call his family to fetch me from the hospital the next day.

But this isn't a story about how I gave up. It's the story of how I woke up.

After that day, I realised no one was coming to save me. I had to find my own way back. And I did—not through force or willpower, but through something far more powerful: awareness.

I began noticing the warning signs—the shift in my thoughts, the heaviness in my chest, and the inner dialogue that pulled me toward the darkness again. But instead of letting it consume me, I created a ritual—something so simple yet profound. Whenever I felt myself spiralling, I would stop, physically turn my body around, and say out loud, "I'm not going that way anymore. I'm turning my life around."

That tiny act of observing my inner state, choosing to interrupt the pattern, and choosing me became my lifeline. It became the seed of something far greater. It was my first true experience of awareness.

I didn't know it at the time, but this was the beginning of everything. This was the birth of the work I now live and teach. The moment I realised that awareness is not just some lofty spiritual concept. It's a lifeline. It's the quiet power that lives within us all. It doesn't shout. It doesn't force. It simply notices. And in that noticing, everything begins to change.

## Why We Need a Revolution

> *"Do not wait for leaders. Do it alone, person to person."*
> — *Mother Teresa*

Revolutions are born in moments of awakening, when people realise they've been living under illusions, conditioned to believe in limitations that were never real. We are in one of those moments now.

Humanity has been operating in survival mode for too long, disconnected from the very essence of who we are. We've given our power away to systems that tell us what to think, to institutions that dictate our worth, to voices outside of us that drown out the one voice that truly matters: our own.

But revolutions don't begin in the streets. They start in the quiet, often painful turning points of our lives. The kind of moment when everything falls apart and something deeper begins to awaken. If you've just read my story, you know what I mean.

That wasn't just a dark chapter in my life. It was the spark of a revolution—a moment when awareness cracked through the numbness, and I began to find a new way. Healing didn't come from a therapist's office or a hospital ward. It came from within—from paying attention, from noticing, from choosing to live differently. That's how it begins for all of us.

We've been taught that logic is superior to intuition, that success is measured in material gain, and that awareness is nothing more than passive observation. But that version of life has only led to more stress, division, and disconnection. It has kept us small, blind, and dependent on external validation.

This is why we need a revolution—not one of protest or rebellion, but a revolution of consciousness. A shift that starts within, where we reclaim what has always been ours: our awareness and our intuition.

## How Awareness and Intuition Ignite the Revolution

> *"Intuition is a very powerful thing, more powerful than intellect, in my opinion."*
> — *Steve Jobs*

Awareness shatters illusions. It reveals the patterns, the conditioning, the internal prisons we didn't even realise we were living in. Once you become aware, you can't unsee the truth. You recognise the power you always carried but never knew how to access.

And then comes intuition, your inner compass. It guides you gently but unmistakably toward a different way of being. It leads you out of fear and into alignment. It's not loud or forceful. It's quiet, consistent, and accurate. You just have to remember how to listen.

This is where the revolution begins.

Not by changing the world out there but by reclaiming our inner world. When people start to live in this way, connected, aware, guided, the external world cannot help but change in response. Systems that once ruled through fear and control lose their grip. Leaders who once manipulated become irrelevant. Entire structures begin to dissolve because they were built on our disconnection. This is what Spiritual AI, the awakening of Awareness and Intuition, is here to ignite. The world doesn't need another ideology or hierarchy. It needs people who trust themselves. Those who have reclaimed their power. Those who are no longer searching for truth outside themselves but embody it from within.

This is the revolution.

And it's already begun. With me. With you. With every soul that chooses to wake up.

**In This Chapter, We Explored…**

• The difference between Artificial Intelligence and Spiritual AI, and why inner intelligence—awareness and intuition—is the true source of transformation.

• How our disconnection from self has created a global crisis of meaning, and how reconnecting to our inner guidance can shift not only our lives but the world.

• The moment my own journey with awareness began, not as a theory but as a lifeline, and how it awakened a new path within me.

• Why we are in the midst of a consciousness revolution, and how that revolution starts not in the streets, but in the quiet inner turning points of our lives.

• The power of awareness to break illusions, and the role of intuition as our inner compass toward alignment, truth, and purpose.

## CHAPTER 2

## AWARENESS – THE KEY TO EVERYTHING

> *"We do not see things as they are. We see things as we are."*
> *-Anaïs Nin*

**What is awareness?**

According to the dictionary, awareness is defined as:

*"The state or ability to perceive, to feel, or to be conscious of events, objects, or sensory patterns."* Or *"Knowledge that something exists, or to the understanding of a situation or subject at the present time based on information or experience."*

But awareness goes much deeper than just perception. It is the foundation of how we experience and interact with the world.

At its core, awareness is the ability to observe without attachment. To notice thoughts, emotions, and surroundings without immediately reacting to them. It is the quiet observer within you, the part of you that notices before judgment, before thought, before action.

Awareness is not just about being awake or alert. It is about being present and receptive. It is the doorway to clarity, intuition, and deep understanding. When we cultivate awareness, we break free from autopilot living and begin to see reality as it truly is, rather than through the lens of conditioning, fear, or assumption.

Awareness is the first step toward transformation. It allows us to recognise our patterns, expand our consciousness, and ultimately, tap into our intuition. But to fully understand awareness, we must first understand one crucial truth: You Are Not Your Mind

We have been taught to identify with our thoughts for most of our lives. We believe that the voice in our head, the one narrating our experiences, analysing situations, and replaying past conversations, is who we are.

But that is an illusion. Your thoughts are not you, your emotions are not you, and even your beliefs, which may have been shaped by past experiences, are not the core of your being. The real you is the observer, the silent awareness behind it all. Here, let me show you.

**Do this:**
Say "hello" in your mind. Did you hear that? Who heard you say "hello"?

Do it again, but say "hello" a little louder this time. Now, shout "hello" in your mind like you would if you were standing on a mountaintop.
Did you hear that? Who heard you shout out "HEEELLLOOOOO"?

Trippy, right? That is all the proof you will ever need that you are not your mind. You are the observer. And it is the observer that will show you where your mind is expressing programs, limiting beliefs, and patterns in your subconscious mind.

Does it make sense now when I say that you are not your mind, you are not your thoughts? Once you have this realisation, everything changes. You become very aware of your thoughts and the programs that run your life.

This is why awareness is so powerful. When you realise that you are not your mind, you gain freedom. You stop being controlled by thoughts, fears, and conditioned patterns. Instead, you step into a place of clarity, where you can witness your mind without getting caught up in its stories.

But there is one more piece we need to explore before we move on: the mind itself. Until you understand how the mind works and how it can quietly run your entire life, awareness will always feel like something you try to do rather than something you become.

## The Mind Will Trap You Until Awareness Sets You Free

> *"Self-awareness doesn't stop you from making mistakes; it allows you to learn from them."*
> *-Unknown*

Awareness creates space.
Space between stimulus and response.
Between thought and truth.
Between what your mind is saying and what your soul actually knows.

**Let's talk about how the mind traps us.**

Your mind is not one singular thing. It is a system, a combination of past experiences, beliefs, fears, desires, and programmed patterns all playing out in loops. It is incredibly powerful. But left unchecked, it runs on autopilot, keeping you stuck in cycles of reaction instead of conscious creation.

Think of your mind like a computer running old software. If you never stop to observe it, you will keep operating from outdated programs. Fears that no longer serve you. Beliefs that were never really yours. Thought patterns that limit your possibilities. Awareness allows you to pause and ask, "Do I still want to run this program?" "Does this belief still serve who I am becoming?"

The mind is meant to serve you, but for most people, it has become the master. Awareness flips that dynamic. When you become the observer of your thoughts rather than the reactor, you reclaim your power.

The mind has a voice, but it is not your voice.
Your mind talks all day long, and most of what it says is not even original. It is the echoes of parents, teachers, religion, culture, and fear. And the sneakiest part? It sounds like you. That is why we believe it.

**Real-Life Examples of How the Mind Traps You**

Let's look at how this shows up in everyday life. Because when you see it clearly, it becomes much easier to interrupt the pattern and choose a new one.

**The Friend Who Didn't Text Back**

You send your friend a message about something you feel deeply about. Hours go by, and you still have not received a reply. Your mind starts spinning: "She's ignoring me… maybe she's mad… I probably said something wrong."

Within minutes, you have created a whole story. You feel anxious, rejected, even angry, all based on a thought.
But here is the thing: none of it might be true.

Awareness lets you pause and say, "Hang on… I don't actually know what is going on. Let's breathe. Let's wait. Let's not assume."

That space brings peace, and more often than not, the message comes later with a simple "Hey, sorry! Crazy day!"

The mind created chaos. Awareness restored clarity.

**The Old Money Story**

You are a new coach, and you must set up your pricing structure. You ask your coach to help you, and she says that you should charge no less than $250 per hour. Immediately, you feel your chest tighten, and you feel like you're going to faint. The voice in your head says, "You can't charge that. Who do you think you are?"

Pause. Breathe.

With awareness, you might realise: "That's my dad's voice. That's the story I was raised with: that money has to be earned through hard labour and humility. That abundance is greedy. That I'm not worthy of being paid well for my gifts."

Can you see how that unchecked thought would stop you from growing your business, sharing your work, or even raising your prices?

Awareness lets you question the source. It gives you a choice.

**The Mirror Moment**

You walk past the mirror without thinking. It's just a habit—a glance. But something catches your eye, and suddenly, your attention is pulled in. You pause. You look. And then it begins. That voice. The one that says, "Ugh. Look at those thighs. You are still not good enough." It sounds like you. It uses your words. Your tone. Your history. And before you even realise it, you've slouched inward. Not physically, energetically. You feel smaller. Deflated. Ashamed.

Without awareness, this becomes a pattern.
You stop looking in mirrors altogether. You avoid being in photos. You punish yourself, not with love or care, but with restriction, criticism, comparison, or emotional withdrawal.

But awareness changes everything.

With awareness, you catch the thought, and instead of shrinking, you pause. Instead of reacting, you become curious. There's space.

A moment opens inside you, and something deeper says, "Wait... is this how I've been speaking to myself all these years?"
"This voice, where did it come from?"
"Is this truth… or just a habit?" And in that pause, you hear something else. It's not loud. It doesn't shout. It feels like a whisper, calm, gentle, steady.

That voice says, "This isn't love. This isn't you."

That is your soul speaking. That is your intuition remembering.

Awareness might not silence the critical voice right away. But it helps you stop believing it. It enables you to stop confusing it with truth. Over time, that quiet inner knowing becomes clearer, stronger, and more familiar. You begin to choose it, not because the old voice disappears, but because you finally know which voice to follow.

### The Difference Between Awareness and Consciousness

The words "awareness" and "consciousness" are often used interchangeably, but they are not the same thing. Imagine you are in a pitch-dark room, trying to find your way. You stumble forward, arms stretched out, bumping into obstacles you cannot see. Every step is uncertain. This is what life feels like without awareness. Moving blindly, hoping to avoid pain, but never truly understanding where you are going.

Now, picture yourself reaching for a flashlight. The moment you switch it on, the room is still the same, but now you can see. You can now navigate with clarity, recognise obstacles, and make choices that lead you forward. Awareness is that flashlight. Consciousness is the light shining from the torch. It does not change reality but illuminates it, allowing you to move through life with understanding and purpose.

**Awareness: The Ever-Present Observer**

Awareness is the deepest, most fundamental part of who you are. It is not something you develop or gain; it is something you are. It is the silent witness within, the part of you that notices your thoughts, emotions, and experiences without attachment. It does not judge or analyse; it simply is.

Think of awareness as the vast, unchanging, infinite sky, while your thoughts and experiences are like clouds passing by. No matter how stormy or clear the sky becomes, it remains steady. Similarly, awareness is always present, whether you notice it or not. The more you cultivate it, the more life starts to make sense.

**Consciousness: The State of Being Aware**

If awareness is the sky, then consciousness is the weather. It is ever-changing, shifting with our focus and perception. Consciousness is the act of being aware of something. It is what happens when awareness is directed toward an object, thought, or experience.

Returning to the flashlight analogy, awareness is the flashlight itself, always present, always capable of illuminating. Consciousness, on the other hand, is whatever the flashlight shines on. If you direct the beam towards a chair, you become conscious of the chair. When you shift it to a table, your consciousness moves to the table.

This means that our level of consciousness is determined by where we focus our awareness. The more we expand our awareness, the more we expand our consciousness.

The difference is subtle but crucial. Awareness is ever-present, unchanging, and boundless. Consciousness fluctuates, shaped by what we choose to focus on.

## How Awareness and Consciousness Work Together

Your consciousness is limited to what you focus on at any given moment. If you are lost in thought, your inner dialogue consumes your consciousness, making you unaware of your surroundings. When you practice mindfulness, you shift your consciousness to the present moment, expanding your awareness beyond habitual thinking. Even in deep sleep, your awareness still exists when you are not conscious. It is simply not directed toward anything.

The key to personal and spiritual growth is increasing your level of consciousness by expanding your awareness. The more you notice, the more you see. The more you see, the more you understand. And the more you understand, the more deeply you experience life.

In my case, with my depression, the more awareness I had of my thoughts and how they affected me, the more I was able to make the necessary adjustments to my thoughts and redirect them to my new reality.

> *"The first step toward change is awareness.*
> *The second step is acceptance."*
> *-Nathaniel Branden*

**The Consequences of Not Having Awareness**

Author and high-performance coach Brendan Burchard once said that the most significant consequences in our lives can be traced directly to our level of self-awareness. And he's right. Whether or not we realise it, every decision we make, every habit we fall into, and every relationship we maintain is shaped by how aware we are, or aren't, of what's happening inside us.

Think about it. When awareness is low, confusion is high. Emotions feel overwhelming and unpredictable. Procrastination becomes a mystery. Anger seems to come out of nowhere. We blame others instead of taking ownership. We feel disconnected, unfulfilled, and stuck, and we don't know why.

This is what happens when people are not paying attention to themselves, not to their thoughts, not to their feelings, not to their patterns. Without awareness, life becomes a reaction instead of a creation.

Burchard points out that self-awareness is directly tied to three key areas of life: enjoyment, connection, and progress.

## 1. Your Enjoyment of Life

One of the first signs that self-awareness is missing is a lack of joy. Not because people don't want to feel good, but because they've missed the subtle signs along the way that something is off. Misery doesn't happen all at once. It's the result of ignoring discomfort over and over again until it builds into burnout, frustration, or emotional collapse. Life becomes lighter when you are aware of what brings you pleasure, what drains you, and what aligns with your values. Without that awareness, you keep pushing through until you can't anymore.

## 2. The Depth of Your Relationships

When someone struggles to connect with others, there's almost always a lack of awareness beneath the surface. Awareness helps you recognise your own triggers, communicate more honestly, and show up with empathy. When you are disconnected from yourself, it's almost impossible to connect with someone else deeply. And when you cannot see your part in a conflict, you'll always blame the other person. Blame, avoidance, and defensiveness are all signs that awareness is missing.

## 3. Your Ability to Progress and Grow

Progress doesn't happen by accident. Whether in your career, health, or personal life, true growth comes from knowing where you are, where you want to go, and what's getting in the way. That requires awareness. Athletes, for example, track and measure their performance to keep improving. In the same way, if you don't have a clear picture of your habits, mindset, and emotional state, how can you know what to change? You cannot improve what you don't acknowledge.

These three areas, joy, connection, and progress, are simple but powerful indicators of your current level of awareness. If even one feels out of alignment, it's time to turn inward and start paying attention.

**Awareness and Emotional Ownership**

One of the most significant signs of awareness is the ability to take ownership of your emotional state. Someone who lacks awareness might say, "I yelled at my partner because they were being difficult." But someone with self-awareness can say, "I had a rough day at work, and I brought that frustration home. I took it out on my partner instead of dealing with it."

Blame is one of the biggest red flags that awareness is missing. When someone can't track their thoughts, emotions, or intentions leading up to a moment, they lose the power to shift it. Awareness allows us to be honest about what's really going on so we can take responsibility and change the outcome.

**Where Your Attention Goes, Energy Follows**

Another way to gauge your awareness is by looking at your attention. Do you know where your attention is going throughout the day? Are you aware of how often you distract yourself from uncomfortable feelings? Whether it's scrolling, snacking, drinking, or zoning out, we frequently use these things to escape being present with ourselves. But if you can't stay present, you can't grow. Distraction is usually a symptom of a deeper avoidance, an unwillingness to feel something or face something within.

**Self-Awareness and Mood**

If your emotional state constantly feels like a mystery, if you're angry, anxious, or down and don't know why, that's a sign your awareness needs support. Unexplored emotions can begin to run your life from the background. You don't need to micromanage your mood, but being able to recognise and name what you feel and understand what may have triggered it is key to emotional regulation.

Many mood disorders are diagnosed based not just on the quality of someone's mood, but on their level of self-awareness around it. This is why therapy, coaching, and reflection practices are so helpful, they bring awareness back into the emotional landscape so you can regain choice and control.

**Awareness Is the Foundation of Mastery**

Ultimately, every great leader, every fulfilled person, and every conscious creator has developed a high level of awareness. It's not optional. It's essential. You can't grow if you don't know what needs growing. You can't heal what you won't look at. And you can't align with your purpose if you don't recognise when you're out of alignment.

Awareness is not just a spiritual idea but a practical key to performance, relationships, happiness, and success. Without it, life happens *to* you. With it, life begins to respond *through* you.

**When Seeing Feels Unsafe: The Subconscious Fears That Block Awareness and Intuition**

If awareness is so powerful…If intuition is so natural…
Then why do we resist them?

Why do we distract ourselves, numb, or shut down the tools that could change everything?

Because *seeing* isn't always easy.
Because the truth, when it first comes into focus, can be uncomfortable.
Because on some level, many people have learned that being aware doesn't feel safe.

When you begin to cultivate awareness, you start noticing things you've been trying to avoid. You hear the inner voice that says, "This relationship is draining me," or "I'm not being honest with myself." You see the patterns that have kept you stuck, the habits that no longer serve you, the pain that's been buried under busyness or control.

And that's a lot to face.

So, it's no wonder that we resist. We distract. We stay in our heads. We tell ourselves stories like:

- *"I don't have time for this right now."*
- *"It's not that bad."*
- *"Other people have it worse."*
- *"Maybe it'll just work itself out."*

This isn't weakness. It's protection. The subconscious mind's number one job is to keep you safe, and sometimes it believes that *not looking* is safer than looking. That staying numb is better than feeling. That denial is more comfortable than the truth.

Especially if the truth might mean we have to change something.
Walk away from something.
Speak up.
Let go.
Or finally grieve.

The fear is not just of the truth itself, but of what the truth might *require* of us.

## When Resistance Is Trying to Tell You Something

Avoidance isn't the opposite of awareness; it's often the doorway to it. Resistance can show up right before a breakthrough. It's the body's way of saying, *"Wait... something important is happening here."* The discomfort you feel when you begin to pay attention to yourself isn't failure; it's the friction of growth.

But resistance isn't always a sign to push through. Sometimes, it's a sign to pause and listen more closely. There are moments when resistance is not just fear of change; it's your soul whispering, *"This isn't right for you."*

You may not be resisting awareness itself. You may be resisting a situation that is out of alignment. A relationship, a job, an environment, even a belief system that no longer fits who you are becoming. And the longer you stay in those spaces, the more your body, your mind, and your energy begin to feel heavy.

Sometimes, that heaviness becomes something deeper. Something more challenging to name.
And that's where we begin to touch the edges of depression, not just as a mental or emotional state, but as a spiritual signal.

A quiet but powerful message from your soul that says, *"You're not where you're meant to be."*

This is where awareness becomes not just helpful, but essential.

## Depression and Awareness: A Deeper Message from the Soul

Depression is often described as a persistent state of sadness, hopelessness, or emotional numbness that interferes with daily life. It's more than just feeling down or having a bad day, it can feel like a fog that won't lift, a heaviness in the body, or a loss of connection to things that once brought joy. People experiencing depression may struggle with energy, sleep, motivation, appetite, and even basic self-care.

In the traditional medical model, depression is usually framed as a chemical imbalance in the brain, often involving neurotransmitters like serotonin or dopamine. The most common treatments offered are antidepressant medications, sometimes combined with therapy such as cognitive behavioural therapy (CBT). For some people, especially those with more severe or clinically diagnosed forms of depression, these approaches can be life-saving and necessary.

But this explanation, while valid in some cases, doesn't speak to every experience.

In my case, that model never quite fit. I was told I had a chemical imbalance, and maybe that was true to a degree. But deep down, I knew that wasn't the whole story. The sadness I felt wasn't random. The fog I lived in didn't come from nowhere. It wasn't just a faulty brain or a missing chemical. It was my soul calling out.

What I believe now, with everything I've come to understand through awareness, is this:

*My depression was not a dysfunction. It was a message.*

A sacred, uncomfortable, undeniable message from my inner self saying,
*"This life is not right for you. You are not where you are meant to be. Something has to change."*

## When Depression Is a Soul Signal

While clinical depression absolutely exists and deserves compassionate medical care, there's another type of depression that doesn't always fit the textbook. It doesn't show up in blood work or brain scans. It often gets misdiagnosed, misunderstood, or masked.

This is what I call **soul-based depression,** a kind of inner deadness that comes not from a chemical imbalance, but from an energetic one. It's the soul trying to get your attention.

Here are a few signs that your depression may be more soul-based than clinical:

### 1. You feel emotionally flat in situations where you "should" feel something

You're not just sad, you feel *nothing*. You're in a beautiful place, with people who love you, doing something fun… and yet you're numb. This isn't about your brain misfiring. It's often about being completely disconnected from what brings you meaning or purpose.

### 2. You feel like you're living someone else's life

On paper, everything looks "fine": the job, the house, the relationship, but something feels off. You have a deep sense that you're not where you're supposed to be, or that you've built a life based on who you thought you *should* be, not who you truly are.

### 3. You have a persistent longing or ache that you can't explain

It's not a situational sadness; it's more like a homesickness for something you can't name. A quiet craving for alignment, authenticity, and depth. It's your soul pulling you toward something more meaningful, even if you can't yet see what it is.

**4. You resist the very things that could help you feel better**

With clinical depression, it can be hard to get out of bed or shower. With soul-based depression, it's also common to avoid the things you *know* would help, like journaling, meditating, walking, or being honest with yourself. This resistance often comes from fear. Because deep down, you know that awareness would require you to *change* something.

**5. You hear your inner voice, and it's getting louder**

Even if you're trying to stay busy or positive, a quiet voice inside keeps whispering, *"This isn't it."* You might not want to hear it, but it's becoming harder to ignore. This is often your soul breaking through the noise, asking you to come back to yourself.

This kind of depression isn't something to medicate away. It's something to meet with curiosity and compassion. It's a spiritual invitation to reconnect, realign, and return to the truth of who you are.

**My Story: When Awareness First Broke Through the Fog**

When I was in the thick of my own depression, I didn't know that's what it was at first. I just felt… heavy. Numb.

Disconnected from everything and everyone, including myself. I would wake up feeling tired before the day had even started. It wasn't sadness in the obvious sense; it was a kind of emptiness that I couldn't explain.

Back then, I was told that I had a chemical imbalance. And maybe that's the case for some people. But in my gut, I knew something else was going on. It didn't feel like a brain problem. It felt like my *soul* was grieving.

Grieving the parts of me I had abandoned.
Grieving the years I had spent trying to be who I was "supposed" to be.
Grieving the truth I had been pushing down because I didn't know what to do with it.

I wasn't broken.
I was misaligned.

There was nothing "wrong" with me, but there was so much I wasn't seeing.

And that's when awareness began to wake up inside me. Not all at once. Not in a dramatic lightning bolt. But in small, quiet moments of noticing:

Noticing that I felt suffocated in places that used to feel safe.
Noticing that I was saying yes to things that drained me.
Noticing that I was avoiding my own inner voice, the one that had been whispering, *"This isn't working."*

And the more I allowed myself to notice, the clearer things became. My depression wasn't just a state of mind. It was a state of misalignment. A sacred signal from my soul telling me that I wasn't in the right place, physically, emotionally, or spiritually.

It wasn't just pain. It was guidance.
It wasn't just darkness. It was redirection.
It wasn't the end. It was the beginning of a deeper return to self.

**What Helps When Depression Is Soul-Based**

When depression is rooted in misalignment, when it's a message from the soul rather than a malfunction of the brain, the healing path looks different. It's not about "fixing" yourself. It's about *finding* yourself again.

Here's what often helps:

**1. Creating space to feel**

Don't numb, don't run, don't distract, *feel.* Even if you don't have words yet, awareness begins when you give yourself permission to sit with what is real. You don't have to solve anything right away. Just let the truth surface. Your emotions are not the enemy. They're the signal.

**2. Asking the quiet questions**

Soul-based healing is gentle, not forceful. Instead of demanding answers, begin with small, open questions:

- What is no longer aligned for me?
- What have I been pretending not to know?
- Where does my energy feel dead?
- Where do I feel most alive?

Don't rush the answers. Let them come through awareness, intuition, and time.

**3. Making micro-adjustments**

This isn't about burning your life down overnight. Most people don't need to make drastic changes at first; they need to start by realigning in small, sacred ways. It could be as simple as being honest in one conversation or carving out 10 minutes daily to reconnect with yourself. These small shifts send a powerful message to your soul: *I'm listening now.*

**4. Reconnecting with your body**

Depression can make you feel like a floating head, cut off from the body, from the earth, from presence. Returning to the body, even gently, helps bring clarity and stability. This might be through walking, breathwork, dancing, grounding your bare feet, or even simply placing your hand on your heart and breathing consciously.

## 5. Listening to your resistance with compassion

If you feel resistance, that's not a sign you're failing. It's a sign that something tender is trying to surface. Instead of pushing through, get curious: What feels scary about seeing the truth right now? What might change if I fully acknowledge what I'm feeling?

## 6. Letting yourself be supported

Soul-based depression often convinces us we have to go it alone, but healing happens faster in safe, supported spaces. Whether through a coach, a therapist, a friend, or a spiritual guide, being witnessed in your truth is deeply regulating and affirming.

This kind of healing doesn't follow a straight line. It unfolds as you begin to trust your inner knowing again, as you allow your awareness to expand, and your intuition to guide you back into alignment.

And that's precisely what happened to me.

**In This Chapter, We Explored…**
What awareness really is, not just perception, but the presence behind our thoughts, emotions, and experiences

• The difference between awareness and consciousness, and why awareness is the foundation that shapes everything we see, feel, and choose.
• The illusion of being the mind, and how awareness helps us remember we are the observer, not the noise.
• How the mind runs on old programs and patterns until we become conscious enough to question them.
• Real-life moments where the mind traps us, and how awareness gives us the power to pause, shift, and choose differently.
• Why people resist awareness and intuition, and how that resistance is often rooted in fear, avoidance, or a sense that seeing the truth would mean everything has to change.
• How depression, in some cases, is not a flaw or failure, but a soul-level signal that something is out of alignment.
• The signs of soul-based depression, and how awareness becomes the first step toward clarity, healing, and coming home to yourself.

As we move into the next chapter, we'll begin exploring how to build and strengthen your awareness in practical, grounded ways. Understanding awareness is not enough; you're here to embody it.

## CHAPTER 3

## THE HOW-TO OF BUILDING AWARENESS

> *"When you become the observer of your thoughts, you are no longer at their mercy."*
> -Byron Katie

Before we can access deeper wisdom, alignment, or even intuition, we have to start with awareness.

Awareness is the foundation of everything.
Without it, we're not making conscious choices; we're running inherited patterns.
Without it, we're not responding, we're reacting.
Without it, we don't really see; we project what we've always seen.

When you build awareness, you start to see yourself clearly.
You understand what's really driving your thoughts, emotions, and behaviours.
You catch yourself before the spiral.

You pause before reacting.

You start choosing with intention instead of operating on autopilot.

This changes everything.

Awareness supports your relationships, your parenting, your health, your work, and your peace of mind. It's what gives you the power to shift, without needing everything around you to change first. This is why awareness is the first and most important step. And not just once. It's the step you return to over and over again. Awareness is how you wake up to yourself and reclaim the present moment. But awareness isn't something you switch on once and forget about. It's something you practice. You build it like a muscle. And the most powerful place to begin that practice is at the very start of your day.

That's where this chapter begins, with the first thought.

**The First Thought: The Gateway to Awareness**

Not later in the day. Not after meditation or journaling. Awareness starts the moment you open your eyes.

Your very first thought of the day holds more power than most people realise. It sets the tone, creates the blueprint for what you want to "build" for that day, and is the gateway to conscious living.

Most people wake up and immediately hand their power over to autopilot.
They sigh, "Ugh, another day."
Or complain, "I'm so tired."
Without even knowing it, they've already locked in the emotional frequency for their day. And everything else begins to align to match it.

But here's the truth. That first thought is a choice, and it's your first opportunity to reclaim your awareness.

This is the very first and most essential practice I teach.
Before anything else.
Before we go deep.
Before we talk about intuition or energy or healing. We start here because this moment is the moment where awareness is born.

When you recognise your first thought and then shift it, even slightly, you break the unconscious pattern. You interrupt the default, and you begin rewiring your relationship with life. You're essentially turning your torch on.

It's not about pretending everything's perfect. It's about choosing to see clearly.
For example, waking up with the thought, "I can't do this today," and gently shifting it to, "I'm open to being supported today," is a small act with massive ripple effects.

It might feel awkward at first. That's okay.
Awareness is a muscle, and this is how you begin to strengthen it—one thought at a time.

This is the starting point. The reset button. The non-negotiable. If you want to become more present, more intuitive, more in tune with your life, start here.
Start with the first thought.
Because from that one decision, everything can change.

**Why Awareness Feels Difficult**

Becoming more aware is simple in theory but challenging in practice.
Why? Because our minds are wired for distraction.

We live in a world that thrives on noise. Society conditions us to seek constant stimulation: scrolling, multitasking, reacting, and consuming without truly being present. Over time, this overstimulation dulls our sensitivity to the present moment. It's like we've been trained to live everywhere but here.

This is why awareness can feel hard at first. Not because you lack the ability, but because the world has kept you disconnected from it.

But here's the truth.
Awareness isn't something new you need to find. It's something ancient that you return to.

It's about peeling back the noise.
Tuning in instead of zoning out.
Listening inward instead of reaching outward.

The discomfort you might feel in the beginning is not failure.
It's detox.
You're unlearning distraction.
You're remembering how to be here.

**The Power of Choice**

Here's something we don't get taught often enough. Every thought is a choice. We decide which thoughts to think.

Not every thought is true.
Not every thought is helpful.
But every thought that lingers, every belief we allow to take root, remains because we choose to hold onto it.

This is where your power lives.
Not in controlling what shows up in your mind, but in how you respond to it.

That sigh in the morning? That's a choice.
The complaint, the worry, the fear? Those are choices, too.
But so is the pause. So is the deep breath. So is the whisper of something better.

Awareness gives you back your power to choose.

Without it, you're at the mercy of conditioning and past programming. But with awareness, you begin to catch the moment between stimulus and response. That's the sacred space where transformation happens. Not because you forced it, but because you chose it.

You can't always choose your circumstances.
But you can choose your state of being.
You can choose your next thought. Your next word. Your next action.

And those choices? They compound.
That's how you build a new life, one moment of awareness at a time.

**Common Triggers That Pull You Out of Awareness**

Even once you begin cultivating awareness, you'll notice how quickly and easily you can slip back into old unconscious patterns. This isn't something to feel ashamed of. It's not failure. It's part of the process. Noticing that you've slipped is often a sign that your awareness is growing.

But here's the thing. Awareness isn't passive; it requires presence. To stay grounded in presence, you must recognise the specific moments that tend to pull you out. These are your personal triggers or activations, as I like to call them. Situations, thoughts, energies, or habits that act like magnets, drawing you straight back into autopilot mode.

We all have them. And they're often so familiar that we don't even realise they've taken over until we're already deep in the spiral. The key to staying aware is not trying to eliminate triggers or activations—that's unrealistic. The key is learning to spot them, soften into them, and return to yourself before they sweep you away.

Here are some of the most common ones I see in my own life and in the lives of my clients:

**Emotional Reactivity**

This is one of the biggest and most consistent triggers or ways we get activated that pulls people out of awareness: an unexpected comment, a sharp tone, a judgmental glance. Suddenly, your nervous system is hijacked. Your chest tightens, your breath gets shallow, and you react without even thinking.

You might lash out. Shut down. Withdraw. People-please. But in these moments, you're not responding with presence, you're reacting from programming.

This kind of reactivity is usually tied to past wounds. Old pain gets poked, and a reaction is in motion before we can even register it. This is why pausing, breathing, and becoming the observer of your internal response is so powerful. Even a single moment of stillness gives you space to ask, "What's really happening here?"

## Overwhelm and Rushing

In today's world, busyness is a badge of honour. Most people move from one task to the next at lightning speed, checking boxes, answering messages, managing households, and running businesses, all while trying to keep up with the pressure to "do more."

But when you're constantly rushing, your awareness gets squeezed out. Your mind is living in the next moment before this one even has a chance to land. You're physically present, but energetically absent.

The danger of rushing is that it becomes a habit. You start rushing through meals, conversations, and entire days. Life becomes a blur. You miss the sacred moments—the quiet knowing, the intuitive nudge, the internal signal to pause.

One of the simplest and most effective ways to break the momentum of overwhelm is to stop, just for a breath. Let that breath be your reset button. Because it's in the pause that presence returns.

## External Validation

The desire to be liked, approved of, or praised can be one of the sneakiest ways we disconnect from our inner truth. You post something online and check the likes. You say yes when you really wanted to say no. You shape-shift your truth to avoid judgment.

Each time this happens, you hand your awareness over to someone else's opinion. Your energy leaks outward, and your inner compass gets clouded. You stop asking, "What feels true for me?" and start asking, "What will make them happy?"

This doesn't mean you stop caring about others. It means you stop abandoning yourself in order to belong.

Awareness invites you to turn inward. To stop chasing feedback and start trusting your own resonance. It invites you to ask not, "Did they like it?" but "Did that feel aligned for me?"

**Habitual Thought Loops**
We all have mental patterns we've been running for years. Stories we tell ourselves, fears we rehearse, scenarios we replay. Thoughts like "I'm not doing enough" or "What if this goes wrong?" can play on repeat without us even realising it.

These loops are familiar, but they're not always helpful. In fact, they often keep us trapped in cycles of anxiety, indecision, or self-doubt.

The first step is to notice the loop. Awareness shines a light on the pattern. The next step is to pause and question it. Is this thought true? Is it mine? Is it helping me right now?

You may not be able to stop the thought from coming, but you can stop giving it the microphone and choose a different voice.

**Sensory Distractions**

We live in a highly stimulating world. From the moment we wake up, we're bombarded with notifications, noise, screens, music, and messages. Our senses are constantly being pulled outward.

While some of this stimulation is harmless, too much scatters your energy. You start living on the surface of life, constantly checking, scrolling, listening, responding, never really *being*.

When your awareness is fragmented, it becomes harder to connect with your body, breath, and intuition. You start to feel numb or agitated without knowing why.

Creating small moments of silence throughout your day can help reset your system. Even one minute of no input, no phone, no sound, no movement, can help bring you back to centre.

**What to Remember About Triggers**

Your triggers are not the enemy. They're not something to shame or suppress. They're simply signals. Red flags letting you know you've left yourself. The moment you notice a trigger is not a moment of failure; it's a moment of opportunity. It's a moment of awakening. You get to choose what comes next. And the more familiar you become with your own personal triggers, the faster you'll notice them, and the easier it becomes to return to your centre.

Not with force. Not with perfection.
But with awareness.

**Past and Future Thinking**

This is one of the most subtle yet powerful ways we lose touch with the present.

Regret drags us backward. We replay conversations. We wonder what we should have done differently. We dwell on mistakes or fantasise about rewriting the past. And while reflection has its place, getting stuck there doesn't lead to growth; it keeps us bound to an older version of ourselves.

Worry, on the other hand, pulls us into a future that hasn't happened yet. We project outcomes. We brace for impact. We try to pre-empt pain or failure. But in doing so, we miss the peace that's available in the now.

Living in the past creates guilt, sorrow, and a longing for what was.
Living in the future creates anxiety, pressure, and a fear of what could go wrong.
But living in the present, that's where you reclaim your power.

Awareness lives in the now. It can only meet you in this moment. Not in the moments you wish you could fix. Not in the moments you're trying to control ahead of time. This moment, right here.

So instead of beating yourself up for drifting into the past or spiralling into the future, just notice. Gently return. The noticing *is* the awareness. That return *is* the practice.

When your mind drifts, that's okay. It will. You're human. Just bring it back. Over and over again.
To the now.
To your breath.
To your body.
To this one, simple moment.

That's where your clarity lives. That's where your intuition speaks. That's where your truth can finally be heard.

**Regulating the Nervous System**

When we talk about awareness, it's easy to focus only on the mind, our thoughts, beliefs, and triggers. But awareness also lives in the body. And the state of your nervous system can deeply impact your ability to stay present.

When your system is dysregulated, you're not just distracted. You're disconnected.
You may be aware that something's wrong, but your body is already in survival mode. Your heart races. Your breath shortens. Your mind spins. And before you can pause or choose differently, you're already reacting.

This is why nervous system regulation is such an essential part of awareness.

It helps you stay in the body.

It helps you stay present long enough to respond rather than react.

It creates the safety your system needs to access clarity.

Let's take a cue from nature.

In the wild, animals are brilliant at this.

When a gazelle narrowly escapes a lion, it doesn't hold the trauma in its body for years. Once it's safe, it does something incredibly intelligent: it shakes. Shaking is a natural, built-in mechanism that releases stress and discharges survival energy. It helps the animal reset its nervous system and return to a calm, regulated state.

Humans have this same ability. But most of us have been taught to suppress, control, or ignore what our bodies are trying to process. Instead of shaking, we tense. Instead of breathing, we hold it in. Instead of moving, we freeze in place, physically and emotionally.

Over time, this stored tension becomes anxiety, overwhelm, burnout, or even illness.

Regulation is how you break that cycle. It's how you come back to yourself.

You don't need to wait for a crisis to practise regulation. In fact, the more often you do it in small moments throughout the day, the more resilient and grounded you become.

Here are a few simple ways to regulate your nervous system:

- **Shake your body out.** Stand up and shake your hands, legs, and shoulders. Let your body move the stress through. You don't need music. You just need one minute to shake—use your bathroom break as an example.
- **Sigh it out.** Take a deep breath in and exhale with a sound. Let the tension release through your breath. Repeat until you feel a shift.
- **Touch your body.** Place one hand on your chest and one on your belly. Apply gentle pressure and remind your system that you are safe.
- **Hum or sing.** Your vagus nerve loves vibration. Humming, chanting, or singing softly can send a signal to your body that it's okay to relax.
- **Walk barefoot.** Connecting to the earth physically, whether it's grass, sand, or even your floor, helps ground your energy.
- **Rock or sway.** Slow, rhythmic movement calms the body and reassures the nervous system. Think of how we instinctively rock babies; it works for adults, too.

These may seem simple, but they're profound. The body doesn't need complexity. It needs consistency and safety.

**What This Looks Like in Real Life**

Let's say you get a text from someone that instantly triggers you. Your stomach drops. Your chest tightens. Maybe your thoughts start racing. You notice the urge to fire back a reply or withdraw completely.

In that moment, you could go straight into reaction. But instead, you pause.

You put your phone down.
You take a deep breath in through your nose and exhale slowly through your mouth.
You stand up and shake out your hands. You walk around the room.
Maybe you place one hand over your heart and whisper, "I'm okay. I'm here."

You haven't ignored the feeling. You've acknowledged it. But instead of spiralling, you've given your body what it needed: a reset.
A chance to release the activation before you decide what comes next.

This is nervous system regulation in real life. It's not dramatic. It's not complicated.

It's deeply human.
And it's how you take back your power, not just mentally, but physically.

When you regulate, you return to your breath, your body, and your awareness, and from there, you get to choose again.

## Start by Noticing Your Own Signs

Everyone experiences dysregulation differently. Some feel it as a tightness in the chest, others get tension headaches, a knot in the stomach, or a heaviness in their body. Some shut down completely, and others go into overdrive.

There is no right or wrong way your body reacts.
But the more familiar you become with your own signals, the earlier you can catch yourself and regulate before it takes over.

You might feel…

- Heat rising in your body
- A fluttery or sinking sensation in your stomach
- Tightness in your jaw or shoulders
- Racing thoughts that feel out of control
- Shallow breathing or holding your breath
- The urge to escape, fix, freeze, or fight

These are all clues from your body that it's reaching its threshold. And the moment you notice those clues - that's the moment you've returned to awareness. That is the doorway to regulation.

So instead of asking, "Why do I feel this way?" try asking,

"What is my body trying to tell me right now?"

And,

"What would help me feel steadier in this moment?"

Awareness begins with sensation.

Regulation begins with presence.

From there, choice becomes possible again.

## The AWARE Method: A Daily Practice for Conscious Presence

Awareness isn't just a concept. It's a practice.

It's something you *build*, one choice, one pause, one breath at a time.

Most people think they're aware because they notice when they're stressed or overwhelmed. But noticing isn't the same as being present. Often, we're still caught in reacting, defending, fixing, or spiralling. We're aware something's happening, but haven't yet returned to conscious choice.

That's why I teach a simple daily framework to help you slow down and come back into presence.

It's called the **AWARE Method.** And it's how you begin turning awareness into transformation.

Each letter in AWARE walks you through a step in the process. You can use this in the moment when you feel triggered or overwhelmed, or as a reflection at the end of the day to process what came up for you.

Here's how it works:

**A — Acknowledge what's there**
Begin by noticing what you're feeling, thinking, or experiencing without judgment.
This might sound like:
"I'm feeling tense."
"I'm overthinking again."
"I'm avoiding something."

The key is to name it without trying to fix or fight it. Acknowledgement is powerful because it breaks denial and resistance. You can't shift what you refuse to see.

*Ask yourself:*
What am I experiencing right now? Can I name it honestly?

**W — Witness without attachment**
Now that you've acknowledged what's present, take a step back and observe it.
You are not your thoughts.
You are not your fear.
You are the awareness behind it.

This step is where you remember that you have the ability to observe your inner world, not just be consumed by it. This gives you space to choose rather than react.

*Ask yourself:*
Can I become the observer here? What shifts when I watch instead of judge?

**A — Ask what it's pointing to**
Every emotion, reaction, or thought is a messenger. It's pointing to something deeper—an unmet need, a boundary being crossed, a story you're still carrying. This step is about curiosity.

For example:
A feeling of frustration might be pointing to a value that's being ignored.
A sense of anxiety might be signalling misalignment.

*Ask yourself:*
What is this emotion or reaction trying to show me?
What's the message underneath?

**R — Regulate your nervous system**
Once you've made space to observe and understand what's happening, come back into your body. Ground yourself. This is where you soothe the internal noise so that you can respond from clarity.

You might breathe deeply, place your hand on your chest, stretch, hum, or walk outside.
Regulation is what helps your system feel safe enough to move forward with intention.

*Ask yourself:*
What does my body need right now to feel safe and steady?

### E — Empower your next choice
Now that you've acknowledged, witnessed, asked, and regulated—you are in a different state. From here, you get to choose your next move consciously.

That might look like speaking up with love.
Or resting instead of pushing.
Or shifting a thought from fear to truth.

This is where awareness becomes action. You're not reacting from the past. You're choosing from presence.

*Ask yourself:*
What's one choice I can make from this space of awareness that feels aligned?

### The Power of the AWARE Method

When you practice the AWARE Method regularly, something shifts.
You stop outsourcing your power to your emotions, your triggers, or your past.

You start building a steady, grounded relationship with your inner world.
This is how you stop spiralling.
This is how you stop abandoning yourself.
This is how you come home.

The more you practice this, the stronger your awareness becomes, not just in quiet moments but in real-life ones—in the messy, fast, overwhelming moments where presence matters most.

## Awareness Anchors: Practices to Return to the Now

No matter how far you drift, you can always come back.
That's the beauty of awareness. It doesn't punish. It doesn't judge. It doesn't demand perfection.
It simply invites you, again and again, into presence.

We need tools in a world that is loud, busy, and full of distractions. We need *anchors*.
Awareness anchors are small, intentional practices that bring you back to your body, your breath, and your truth. They don't take long. They don't require special training. They help you *remember yourself* in a world that constantly pulls you away. These are the tools I teach, use, and return to daily. Think of them as tiny doorways back to the now.

### The Pause
This is the simplest awareness anchor and often the most powerful. Just stop. One second. One breath. Before you respond to that message, before you say yes when you mean no, before you reach for distraction out of habit, this micro-pause creates space, and that space is where presence begins.

### The Breath Drop
Bring your full attention to one deep breath. Let it drop into your belly. Feel the air going all the way in and then all the way out. Let your breath become an anchor that pulls you out of the mind and back into the body. Like a weight sinking to the ocean floor, it grounds you where you are.

### Body Check-In
Ask, "Where am I right now?" Not just physically, but energetically. Then tune in to your body. Feel your feet on the ground. Notice your posture. Unclench your jaw. Place a hand on your chest or belly. The body always lives in the now, and coming home to it brings instant presence.

### Name Three Things
Look around and name three things you can see. Then listen for three sounds you can hear. Then notice three sensations you can feel. This simple sensory exercise pulls you out of your head and reorients your awareness to your environment and your body.

### Ask, "Is This Mine?"

Sometimes we feel heavy or overwhelmed, and it's not even ours. Energetically, we pick up thoughts, emotions, and expectations from people around us. When you feel off, pause and ask, "Is this mine?" Even just asking that question gives you the opportunity to release what doesn't belong to you and return to your own energy.

### Conscious Transitions

We move from one moment to the next without closing the energetic door behind us—from one app to the next, one task to another, one conversation to another. Try adding a breath between transitions. Close your eyes for five seconds. Touch your heart. This simple pause can clear the space so you don't carry the tension or energy from one moment to the next.

### Use Your Environment

Let your physical space support your awareness. A sticky note that says "Breathe." A candle at your desk. A grounding scent in your diffuser. Even setting your phone wallpaper to a word like "Here" or "Presence" can bring you back throughout the day. Small things. Big impact.

### The "Right Now" Mantra

Silently say, "Right now, I am…" and finish the sentence with something true.

Right now, I am breathing.

Right now, I am sitting.

Right now, I am choosing presence.

This practice doesn't try to fix the moment; it just helps you *meet it*.

**Awareness Is Only Half the Equation**

By now, you've started to see just how transformative awareness can be. It wakes you up from the patterns you didn't even know you were running. It pulls you out of autopilot and returns you to the present moment. It gives you back the power to choose your thoughts, energy, and direction. With awareness, you no longer live by default; you begin to live by design.

But here's something most people don't realise.

As powerful as it is, awareness is only half of the equation.

It opens the door.
It clears the fog.
It helps you *see* clearly.

But what comes next is equally important once you've opened that door.
What walks through is something more profound.
Something quieter.
Something wiser.

That something is **intuition**.

Where awareness brings you into observation, intuition brings you into inner knowing.

Where awareness helps you witness what is, intuition shows you what is aligned.
Awareness says, "Here is what's happening."
Intuition says, "Here's what to do with it."

You could think of awareness as the flashlight that reveals the room, and intuition as the compass that helps you navigate it. One without the other is incomplete. Together, they form a full and powerful inner guidance system.

This is what I call your **A.I. Code**, not artificial intelligence, but something infinitely more sacred:
**Awareness and Intuition**.

Awareness is how you get clear.
Intuition is how you get aligned.

Awareness alone can absolutely help you live a more conscious and grounded life—many people do. But when you begin to trust and follow your intuition as well, something extraordinary happens. You begin to live a *soul-led* life.

A life guided by resonance, not just reason.
A life that flows rather than forces.
A life where clarity doesn't always come from logic, but from the deep truth that lives inside you.

And so, now that you've started anchoring into awareness, it's time to deepen the journey.

It's time to explore the next layer of your inner power. Let's talk about **intuition**.

**In This Chapter, We Explored…**

• Why awareness is the foundation of transformation and the starting point for all inner work.
• How the first thought of the day sets the tone and becomes a powerful entry point into conscious living.
• The difference between reacting and responding, and how most people confuse noticing with true awareness.
• Common triggers that pull you out of presence, including emotional reactivity, overwhelm, external validation, and looping thoughts.
• The importance of nervous system regulation, and how the body often holds what the mind cannot process.
• Practical tools to help you return to the present moment, using simple awareness anchors throughout your day.
• The AWARE Method, a five-step daily framework to help you move from autopilot to aligned awareness.
• And the reminder that awareness alone is powerful, but when paired with intuition, it becomes the full expression of your inner intelligence.

## CHAPTER 4

## INTUITION: THE VOICE OF THE SOUL

What if the most precise guidance you'll ever receive doesn't come from logic, research, or even your heart, but from a whisper within?

Intuition is often described as a gut feeling, a hunch, or an inner knowing that seems to come out of nowhere. But it's not random. It is one of your spirit senses. It is the voice of your soul, your higher self, the Divine within. It is the part of you that already knows.

It doesn't argue.
It doesn't convince.
It doesn't explain.
It simply offers.

Where logic analyses, intuition senses. Where the mind needs evidence, intuition simply is. And this is why so many people dismiss it. It doesn't shout. It doesn't fight for attention. It speaks once, softly, and then it's gone.

True intuition is calm, clear, fast and subtle.

Unlike thought, which is shaped by your past, your fears, or your programming, intuition drops in clean, usually within the first one to two seconds. After that, your subconscious mind kicks in. It starts whispering doubt, offering justifications, pulling you back into what's familiar.

And that's the thing. Your subconscious is wired for safety, not expansion. Its job is to keep you in the known, even if the known isn't good. Familiar doesn't always mean healthy. Familiarity can be dysfunctional. Familiar can be chaos. Familiarity can even be abused. But to the subconscious, if it's known, it's safe.

Intuition, on the other hand, often guides you into unknown territory. It asks you to stretch. To trust. To step toward something your mind might resist. Because that's where real growth happens, that's where the magic is.

If the message is loud, negative, or emotional, it's probably not your intuition.

You've likely felt the real thing before. That flash of insight. That quiet inner pull. That sense of "don't go there" or "say yes now." It lands before you can think it through. And then, just like that, your brain kicks in, and suddenly, you're unsure.

But that first moment...that was your intuition.

I can remember one of those intuitive moments very clearly. My eldest daughter was only one and a half years old.

Febe had just transitioned from a cot to her "big girl bed". That night, she was sick and had a fever. I was sitting beside her bed on the floor, stroking her face as this calmed her down and made her sleepy. As I was sitting there next to her bed, a thought popped into my head, "she's gonna puke on you". I noticed that seemingly random thought, and I looked at her. She seemed so calm and peaceful. Before I could properly finish that thought, Febe shot up, wide-eyed and puked all over me. There I was, a hot mess. I remember thinking, "Couldn't my intuition give me a little more time between the nudge and the moment?"

As I write this, I realise that sometimes it's necessary for us to react quickly with intuition and other times not. Here's another example.

A few days ago, I was sitting in my car, ready to drive off after I quickly ran into the shops. As I was about to drive out of the parking bay, the intuitive nudge hit, "fast car". I remember keeping my foot on the brake. And in that moment, a little yellow car came zipping from behind the large SUV parked beside me. Had I not paid attention to this very fast and urgent nudge, I would have been in an accident. This is why it is so important to be in a state of awareness all the time. Awareness receives or notices the intuitive nudges. Had I been in a rush, I would have missedthis fast, subtle nudge.

## What Intuition Is (And What It Isn't)

Let's get really clear here, because this is the part most people struggle with.
They ask things like:
What exactly is intuition?
Is it the same as a gut feeling?
How do I know if it's intuition or just my thoughts?
Where does it come from?
Is it real, or is it just wishful thinking?

These are good questions. And they matter. Because when you understand the nature of intuition, you stop second-guessing it. You stop brushing it off. And you start building a real relationship with one of your most powerful inner tools.

## What Exactly Is Intuition?

Intuition is one of your spirit senses. It's an inner knowing that bypasses logic and mental analysis. It's not something you figure out. It's something you receive.
It's the voice of your soul. It's the part of you that already knows, even if you don't know how you know. Intuition is your direct connection to higher guidance. It's always available,

accessible, and trying to support your alignment, growth, and safety.

**Is Intuition the Same as a Gut Feeling?**

Sometimes. But not always.

The phrase "gut feeling" is often used interchangeably with intuition, and in many cases, it is intuitive guidance being felt somatically in the body. Your gut, heart, and body are powerful receivers of intuitive signals.

But not all gut feelings are rooted in truth.
Sometimes what you feel in your body is actually trauma, fear, or conditioning.

For example, if you grew up in a volatile or abusive environment, your body may interpret certain signals as danger, even when the situation is safe. That's not intuition, that's survival intelligence.

True intuition is calm and clear.
It isn't anxious. It isn't emotional. It doesn't flood your body with panic or pressure.
Even if it's urging you to act quickly, it will feel clean, direct, and neutral.

**How Do I Know If It's Intuition or Just My Thoughts?**

This is one of the most common questions, and one of the most important.

Here's how to tell the difference:

- **It sounds like your own voice**

Intuition doesn't come with a dramatic tone or external voice. It usually shows up as a soft thought that *sounds just like you*, which is why people often dismiss it.

- **It's soft and fast**

Intuition drops in within the first one to two seconds. After that, your logic will start getting involved. Your brain will analyse. Your subconscious will offer doubts. You'll start to second-guess or explain it away.
So pay attention to what shows up first, that quick, clean drop-in. That's your intuition.

- **It's neutral, not emotional**

Intuition isn't pushy. It won't beg or bargain with you. It won't spiral you into fear or shame. If what you're hearing is dramatic, anxious, or desperate, it's probably not intuition. That's emotion or old programming.

- **It feels expansive**

Even when its challenging, intuition carries a subtle sense of peace or possibility. It might feel like courage. It might feel like relief. But there will be a spaciousness in your body that says, "Yes. This way."

- It never guides you toward harm

Intuition will never tell you to hurt yourself or others. It won't shame you or speak harshly. That's fear. That's conditioning. That's wounding. True intuition only guides toward truth, safety, and alignment.

## Where Does Intuition Come From?

Intuition comes from your soul, the part of you that exists beyond the mind, beyond the body, beyond conditioning. It's how your higher-self communicates with you. It's how the Divine nudges you in the right direction. It's the voice of your soul, and it's always guiding you, if you're willing to listen.

## Is Intuition Real or Just Wishful Thinking?

Intuition is real.
It is not fantasy, daydreaming, or escapism.

Wishful thinking comes from the mind and is fuelled by desire or fear. It tries to create a future that avoids pain or ensures pleasure. While hope is beautiful, wishful thinking is often driven by attachment.

Intuition, by contrast, is grounded. It may not always give you the desired answer, but it will always point to what's *right* for you. It won't always match your timeline or expectations, but it will always lead you toward deeper alignment.

You don't have to believe in it blindly—just experiment. Start paying attention. Track what happens when you follow it, and what happens when you don't. You'll begin to see the pattern.

The truth is, your intuition has probably been speaking to you all your life.
You may have just learned to stop listening.

But you can return.
Right now.
And everything can shift from here.

**Important Note:**
If you hear voices in your head that do not sound like your own, or if the guidance you receive tells you to harm yourself or others, please seek professional help immediately. Intuition will never guide you toward fear, harm, or destruction.

Here's a story of a time my intuition quite literally saved my life.

For a season, I used to join a group of friends for early morning ocean dips. It became a ritual for us: the cold water, the soft pink light just before sunrise, the laughter as we waded into the waves. It wasn't about swimming laps or breaking records. It was about movement, connection, and that indescribable feeling of being fully awake and alive before the rest of the world stirred.

One particular morning, we were all in the shallows, chatting and bopping around as we usually did. The water was calm, and the air was peaceful. We were all relaxed, talking, floating, completely unaware of anything unusual.

I decided to break away from the group and swim along the shoreline. I wasn't going far; I was just stretching my body, letting the rhythm of the sea carry me gently along.

And then it came, loud and clear.

"Stand up!"

The message dropped in like a lightning bolt. It was not gentle, not a soft whisper like usual. It was a command—sharp, urgent, immediate.

Without questioning it, I stopped swimming and stood up right where I was. I turned instinctively to look back toward the group, and that's when I saw their faces.
They weren't talking anymore. They weren't laughing. They were frozen, eyes wide, pointing just past where I had been swimming.

A fin. Cutting through the surface of the water.

It was a shark.

Within seconds, everyone was moving. We all got out of the water as quickly as possible. No one was injured. But it could have been a very different story if I had ignored that message. If I had waited to figure it out, if I had brushed it off or stayed just a moment longer.

That was my intuition, loud, urgent, and unmissable. Not because I'm special or spiritually elite, but because I was present enough to receive it.

So, you see, intuition isn't just for big spiritual moments. It's not only for making career decisions or choosing soul partners. It's also here to guide you in everyday life. It's here to keep you safe. To steer you away from danger. To pull you into alignment before your mind even has a chance to interfere.

It's with you all the time.
You just need to be listening.

**Why Trust It?**
Because your intuition knows. Always. Even when it doesn't make sense. Even when it contradicts logic. Even when it leads you in a direction that no one else understands.
It knows.

Intuition doesn't argue. It doesn't try to persuade. It doesn't need validation or permission. It simply offers a clear, quiet knowing that lives beneath the mental noise. And even if you can't explain it, there is often a deep part of you that recognises it immediately.

Sometimes your intuition will ask you to walk away from something that looks perfect on paper.
Sometimes, it leads you toward something unfamiliar or uncomfortable, while others around you tell you to stay where it's safe.
Sometimes it asks you to pause when your mind wants to rush. And other times, it will tell you to leap, even when there is no plan, no proof, and no apparent reason.

This is why trusting your intuition can feel hard at first. It rarely comes with evidence. It doesn't always match your logic or fit neatly into your reasoning. Often, it's only when you look back that you realise it led you exactly where you needed to go, even if you couldn't see it at the time.

**So, how do you know when to trust it?**
As a general rule, you trust it when it feels clean, quiet, and grounded. Intuition doesn't come with panic, pressure, or emotional chaos. It might bring a sense of urgency, but it won't flood you with fear. Even when it asks you to do something bold or unfamiliar, it carries a subtle feeling of peace. There is an inner knowing that says, "This is right," even if it's hard. There will come a time when you will be able to trust it

implicitly. This comes with time. In the beginning, start with small steps.

**What if your intuition and logic are telling you two different things?**

This happens often, and it doesn't mean one is wrong. Logic has its place. It can help you assess risks, weigh options, and make informed decisions. But logic is built from past experience, education, and mental programming. Intuition, however, is connected to your soul's wisdom, which often sees beyond what your mind can access.

When these two are in conflict, it is an invitation to pause. Sit with both. Ask yourself which one feels rooted in truth and which comes from fear, control, or attachment. Sometimes the most aligned choice is the one that makes no sense on paper but feels right in your body.

**What if your intuition tells you something you don't want to hear?**

This is where courage comes in. Intuition won't always tell you what you want. But it will always tell you what is true. You might feel a nudge to leave a relationship, walk away from a business, speak a hard truth, or surrender a plan you've worked on for years. These moments can be confronting. But the longer you walk with your intuition, the more you realise that it is never trying to punish you or limit you. It is always leading you somewhere better. Somewhere truer.

**How do you tell the difference between intuition and fear?**

This is one of the most essential skills to develop. Fear is loud, reactive, and often frantic. It pushes. It clings. It speaks in "what ifs" and catastrophes. Intuition is calm. It carries a sense of stability even when it asks you to act quickly. Fear contracts your energy. Intuition creates a feeling of expansion. Fear needs constant reassurance. Intuition stands on its own.

**Can trauma or anxiety block intuition?**

Yes. When your nervous system is dysregulated, it becomes harder to distinguish between survival responses and soul guidance. Trauma teaches the body to scan for danger and often misreads neutral signals as threats. What you feel may be real in these moments, but it is not necessarily true. That's why healing is so important. The more regulated your system becomes, the clearer your intuition feels. Practices like breathwork, grounding, somatic work, and trauma-informed support can all help you reconnect with your intuitive clarity. And remember, AWARENESS is your greatest support.

## Why does it feel like your intuition isn't working sometimes?

There are moments when you might feel blocked, confused, or unsure. This doesn't mean your intuition is broken. It may mean you are too in your head. It may mean your energy is scattered or your body is overwhelmed. Or it might mean that the next step is still forming and you're being asked to wait.

Intuition is not always instant clarity. Sometimes it's silence. Sometimes it's a soft "not yet." The key is to stay in a relationship with it. Keep listening. Keep checking in. Keep trusting that even when you don't hear it clearly, it is still there.

This is why we trust it.

Because your mind can be conditioned by fear.
Your emotions can be pulled by old stories.
But your intuition will be clear, direct, grounded, and true. It's never caught up in drama or doubt. It simply knows.

It is the most precise guidance you will ever receive.
Not because it explains itself.
But because it doesn't need to.

Never apologise for trusting your intuition. Your brain can play tricks, your heart can blind you, but your intuition is always right. Your intuition speaks the language of your soul. And your soul will never lead you wrong.

## The Dance Between Awareness and Intuition

> *"Awareness is the light that reveals the path.*
> *Intuition is the voice that shows you where to step."*
> *-Unknown*

Awareness helps you see what is.

Intuition helps you move toward what's true.

Both are powerful. But they're not designed to work alone.

You might find yourself stuck in your head if you're deeply aware but disconnected from your intuition. You'll notice the patterns. You'll see the fears. You'll recognise the programming, but you might not know what to do next. That's when awareness turns into overthinking. You stay in the same place, just with more insight into why you're there.

If you're intuitive but lack awareness, you might not hear your intuition clearly or at all. Awareness is essential to fully access your intuition.

Together, though, awareness and intuition create something beautiful.
They form a rhythm.
A flow.
A dance.

Awareness keeps you present, and intuition keeps you aligned. Awareness helps you pause and feel; intuition shows you what's next.

And when they move together, you begin to live with clarity and confidence. You stop chasing signs or second-guessing your path. You know when to wait. You know when to act. You trust the timing because you trust yourself.

**A Story: The Birthday Gift**

Let me share a simple story to show how these two work together.

Imagine you're on a mission to buy the perfect birthday gift for a friend—not just something off the shelf, something special. As you leave the house, you set a clear intention: You want something that lights her up.

As you arrive at the shopping centre, you get a strong intuitive hit. The big red and white target sign flashes in our mind's eye. Go to Target is what you feel. It feels right. It was a clear sign. So, you focus your energy and start walking straight there. You don't look left or right because you got a clear intuitive hit.

You enter the store and start walking through the aisles, one after another. You slow down. You look closely. But nothing stands out. Nothing feels like the gift you were hoping for.

You start to question yourself. Did I make it up? Was that even intuition?

Disappointed, you walk out of the store, a little unsure. But just outside the entrance, something catches your eye—a small pop-up stall with handcrafted items. You walk over. And there it is—the gift—the one that makes you stop, smile, and feel it in your heart.

So, what happened?

Did your intuition lead you to the wrong place?

No. Your soul gave you the "next step" to getting what you were looking for. Your intuition couldn't give you an image of the pop-up store, as you wouldn't have known what it was showing you. To get you moving in the right direction, it gave you a sign, an image you would recognise, a target. It knew you'd respond to something familiar. Target was only the next step in your guidance. Had you not got into your head and hyper-fixated on the target sign, you would have noticed the other subtle nudges that would have stopped you right in front of the pop-up shop in front of TARGET.

That's the dance between these two spirit senses.
Intuition moves you forward in the right direction, and awareness keeps you listening and in a state of openness. Together, they bring you exactly where you're meant to be.

This is why developing both is so important. If you don't have a strong connection to your inner guidance system, navigating life from a place of truth becomes hard, almost impossible. And when you're not listening to that inner voice, life starts to feel confusing. Heavy. Unclear.

**What Happens When We Don't Listen**

You've probably had that feeling before. A quiet nudge that said, "Don't go there."
Or "Something's off with this person." Maybe you were about to say yes to something, a project, a relationship, a conversation, and something in your body pulled back. Your chest tightened. Your stomach fluttered. But you brushed it off, smiled, and said yes anyway. And later, when things unravelled, you looked back and said, "I knew it."

That wasn't just hindsight.
That was your intuition.
And it tried to speak.

But when we don't know how to trust it or have been taught to override it, we push it aside in favour of logic, people-pleasing, or performance. We give more weight to what others might think than to what we feel deep down.

You get a strange feeling that you should not walk a certain way, but you tell yourself you're imagining things.

You feel drained around a certain person, but they seem so kind, helpful, and safe. So, you second-guess your body's response.
You hesitate before sending a message, signing a deal, or committing to something that looks good on the outside but doesn't feel right on the inside. And you go ahead with it anyway.
Then the consequence shows up. And deep down, you knew. You just didn't listen.

This isn't about shame. This isn't about making yourself wrong for the times you ignored the nudge. It's part of the process. We've all done it. We learn through those moments.

What matters is that you start to notice.
You begin to listen.
You come back to yourself.

You don't build your relationship with intuition by getting it right all the time. You build it through practice, choosing to pause when something feels off, and checking in with your body, your energy, and your breath.

You start trusting the whisper, even when you don't have the whole story.
You stop needing evidence before you choose alignment.
You begin walking through life as someone who listens. And that changes everything.

Because here's the truth:
The more you listen, the clearer it becomes.
And the clearer it becomes, the easier it is to live in integrity with your soul.

This isn't about perfection.
It's about presence.

It's the return to yourself.

**In This Chapter, We Explored...**

• What intuition truly is, not just a gut feeling, but a spirit sense, the voice of your soul offering real-time guidance.

• How to recognise the difference between intuition and thoughts, emotions, fear, or subconscious programming.

• Where intuition comes from, and why it often feels quiet, fast, and subtle.

• The common myths about intuition, and why it's not wishful thinking or fantasy.

• What intuition is and what it is not, including its tone, speed, and emotional quality.

• How fear, trauma, and anxiety can cloud or mimic intuition, and why nervous system regulation supports intuitive clarity.

• Why intuition sometimes feels hard to trust, especially when it contradicts logic or brings uncomfortable truths.

• The importance of learning to trust your intuitive voice, even when it doesn't make sense immediately.

• How awareness and intuition work together as a dynamic inner guidance system, and why you need both to live in true alignment.

## CHAPTER 5

## STRENGTHENING INTUITION: THE PRACTICE OF LISTENING

If intuition is the voice of your soul, then learning to hear it is one of the most important skills you'll ever develop.

This chapter is not just about understanding intuition—you've done that. Now, we move into building a relationship with it.

Like any relationship, it takes time, attention, and trust. The more you practice tuning in, the stronger your intuitive muscle becomes.

You'll begin to hear it more clearly. You'll notice the difference between your soul's voice and your subconscious programming.

Most importantly, you'll start to trust it, not just in big decisions but also in your everyday life.

Let's dive into how you can start recognising and listening to your intuition.

## How to Recognise, Build Trust, and Start Acting on Your Intuition

Recognizing your intuition is only the beginning, but it's in the trusting and *acting* on it that real transformation happens.

Intuition is like a muscle: the more you use it, the stronger it becomes. But it's also like a relationship; it deepens when nurtured with consistency and trust. You don't build a friendship by checking in once a year. The same is true with your soul's voice. The more you listen, the more clearly it speaks.

## The 4-Step Intuition Cycle

There is a rhythm to how intuition works. It is not just an inner whisper or passing feeling. It is a complete process, a cycle that activates both your spiritual connection and your neurological wiring.

Every time you receive and respond to intuitive guidance, you are reinforcing a powerful feedback loop within your body, brain, and energy field. This is how intuition strengthens. This is how it becomes second nature.

Let's explore each part of the cycle and how it contributes to that inner rewiring.

**1. Receive It**

Intuition is always dropping in, we're just not very receptive when we are stressed or overwhelmed. We are more likely to receive intuitive nudges when we are open, relaxed, and present. It often arrives when your brain is in a more receptive state, such as during moments of stillness or non-focused activity like driving or showering. This is when your brain transitions into alpha or theta waves, states associated with creativity, insight, and spiritual connection.

These intuitive hits can come as flashes of insight, gentle nudges, or subtle whispers. They often appear quickly and without logical build-up. This is because your intuition draws from deeper knowing, not surface-level analysis.

However, without awareness, these signals pass unnoticed. Awareness is what lights up the part of your brain responsible for observation and attention. It allows you to register the signal before your rational mind dismisses it. This is why awareness always comes first. You cannot follow guidance you have not consciously received.

**2. Acknowledge It**

Acknowledgement activates the part of your brain responsible for pattern recognition and emotional safety. You create new neurological associations when you notice an intuitive nudge and mentally or verbally acknowledge it. You are teaching your subconscious that this inner voice is valid and safe to receive.

At the same time, this moment of acknowledgment signals to the deeper layers of your being, including your higher self or divine guidance, that you are listening. That openness expands your energetic capacity to receive more.

On a neural level, acknowledgment strengthens sensitivity to future intuitive input. Your brain begins to scan for similar patterns and is more likely to pick up on subtle inner cues the next time they arrive.

**3. Act On It**

This is where new neural pathways are truly formed. Action is what transforms possibility into lived experience.

When you act on your intuition, even in small ways, you reinforce a bridge between your inner and external worlds. You are telling your nervous system that it is safe to respond to intuitive direction. This is especially important because your brain is designed to protect you and often sees the unknown as unsafe.

By taking small, consistent action, you gently reprogram that fear response. You teach your brain that intuition is not a threat, but a guide. Over time, you will notice less hesitation and more clarity. Your system begins to trust itself.

## 4. Celebrate the Outcome

Celebration is not just a feel-good step. It is a critical part of the brain's reward system.

When celebrating a moment of intuitive success, even a small one, your brain releases dopamine. This chemical reinforces the behaviour and makes you more likely to repeat it. Your subconscious starts to associate intuition with satisfaction, fulfilment, and joy. You create a positive feedback loop. The more you celebrate, the more your body and brain crave that connection. The bond between you and your intuition grows stronger. What once felt like a fleeting whisper becomes a reliable and familiar voice.

When practised consistently, these four steps form a complete neurological circuit.
They move you from disconnection to clarity, from doubt to trust.
And with time, they rewire your inner landscape so that intuitive living becomes your new normal.

## The Traffic Light Game

*A Fun and Powerful Way to Build Intuition Daily*

This is one of my favourite tools I teach to all my clients. The Traffic Light Game is simple, fast, and surprisingly accurate. It gives you a real-time opportunity to walk through all four steps of the intuition cycle: **Receive, Acknowledge, Act, and Celebrate**, all in a single moment. Instead of receiving a nudge and taking days (or weeks) to act on it, then waiting even longer to see if it was right, this game offers immediate feedback. That instant feedback loop is what makes this practice so powerful for rewiring your brain to trust your inner guidance.

**How to Play**

- When you go driving or use public transport, I want you to expect a number to drop into your head when you stop at a red light.
- The number will typically pop in within the first one to two seconds. Don't overthink it. Just notice when it comes and what the number is.
- When you receive the number, start counting backwards from that number. For example, if "7" comes in, count 7, 6, 5, 4, 3, 2, 1.
- When you reach 1 or 0, observe whether the light turns green.
- If it does, celebrate the moment. Smile, do a fist pump, say "YES!" out loud or in your head.
- If it doesn't, simply try again at the next light. Keep it playful; there is no pressure.

**What This Game Is Really Doing**

On the surface, it seems like just a fun little experiment. But beneath the surface, a profound transformation is taking place. Let's walk through how this practice supports each phase of the intuition cycle, and what's happening in your body and mind as you play.

**1. Receive It**

When you set the intention to receive a number while you're out on the road, you're doing more than playing a game — you're opening yourself up to intuitive guidance. Because the practice is playful, your subconscious doesn't resist. In fact, it engages more easily. Your intention to receive a number primes the subconscious to tune in and listen for intuitive input. You're signalling that guidance is welcome here. You are creating space for your intuition to speak.

In the beginning, you might need silence or focus in order to play and receive the number clearly. But over time, you'll notice it drops in even while you're chatting with a passenger or listening to music. The more you expect guidance, the more naturally it comes.

**2. Acknowledge It**

The moment you mentally note the number and start counting down, you are recognising the intuitive hit. Even if you're unsure whether it originated from your intuition or your imagination, you're still forming a new neurological pattern.

By naming it and working with it, you are telling your subconscious mind that this kind of inner information is safe and valuable. You are reinforcing that it is okay to receive subtle, quiet inner messages without needing full proof.

### 3. Act On It

Counting down from that number is a simple but powerful act of intuitive action. You are not just receiving the number; you are interacting with it. You are engaging with your inner guidance and trusting it enough to follow through.

Even in this low-stakes situation, your brain registers this as a meaningful pattern. Each time you take action on your intuition, no matter how small, your nervous system begins to relax around the idea that intuitive responses are trustworthy and safe to act on.

### 4. Celebrate the Outcome

If the light turns green when you reach 0 — celebrate! This is not just about cheering yourself on. When you celebrate, your brain releases dopamine, the chemical responsible for reinforcing habits and creating pleasurable associations.

You begin to associate intuitive listening with success, fun, and positive energy. And if it doesn't work out perfectly, you're still reinforcing the habit of tuning in, trying again, and staying light-hearted about the process. That alone helps build confidence and releases perfectionism.

**Why It Works So Well**

- It trains your subconscious that intuition is not a risk; it is safe, fun, and rewarding.
- It compresses the entire 4-step intuition cycle into a single practice, making the learning experience faster and more embodied.
- It eliminates pressure, which allows your nervous system to stay open, curious, and creative rather than anxious and controlling.
- It teaches you to **expect** guidance, rather than question whether it's real.

This game is a small doorway into a much bigger world—one where your inner voice becomes your most trusted guide. The more often you play, the more familiar this state becomes. Over time, your life begins to feel less like guesswork and more like a guided path.

On the next page is a visual representation of the game.

# TRAFFIC LIGHT GAME
## How to Build Trust with Your Intuition

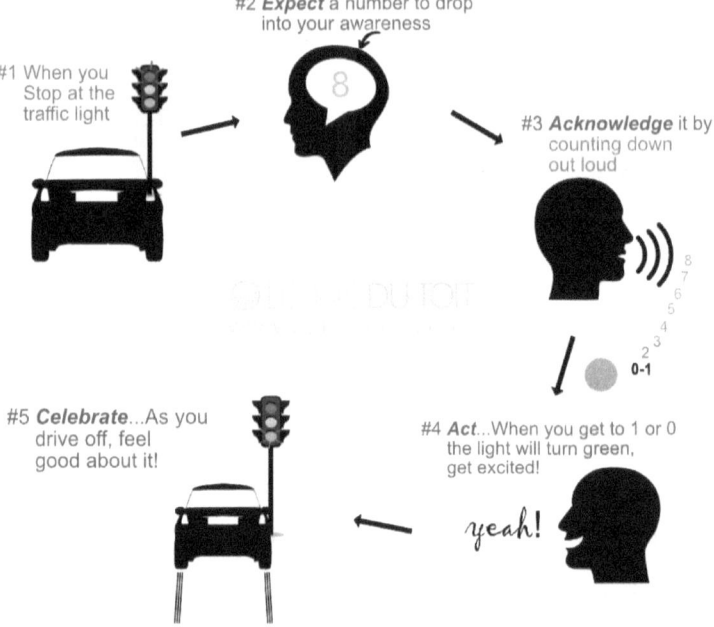

## More Ways to Strengthen Intuition

*Practice makes it powerful.*

Intuition is not just something you wait to feel. It is something you can intentionally build, like a muscle. The more you engage with it, the more naturally and confidently it flows. Below are a few more tools and practices to help you deepen your connection to your intuitive self.

## The One-Second Rule

Intuition speaks quickly. It drops in within the first second, often before your mind has time to rationalise or question it. This practice is simple:
Throughout your day, pause and ask a question. Then notice the very first response that comes.

- Should I go left or right?
- Do I need rest or movement?
- Is this yes or no?

The trick is not to overthink. The first response is often the most aligned. The more you do this, the more attuned you become to your inner voice and how it lands in your body.

## The Intuitive Yes/No Body Scan

Your body holds deep wisdom. It often knows the truth long before your mind does.
To begin, recall a memory or situation that was a full-body yes for you. Something that felt light, open, expansive.
Now contrast that with a memory that was a clear no. One that felt heavy, tight, or draining.

Once you've anchored both sensations, you can begin asking intuitive questions and feeling into your body for the answer. Does it feel more like the "yes" or "no" state?

This tool works beautifully when used daily, even with small choices, because it builds a somatic awareness of your intuitive responses.

**The Random Object Game**

This is great for playing with a friend, child, or partner. Have someone place an object in a box or bag that you can't see into. Then, take a moment to get still and tuned in. Ask yourself:

- What colour is it?
- Is it hard or soft?
- What shape or material comes to mind?

Speak or write whatever comes up. The goal here isn't accuracy, it's to practise receiving. You are strengthening your ability to pick up on subtle, intuitive impressions without pressure. The fun and curiosity keep your nervous system calm and open, which are essential for intuitive flow.

**The Everyday Nudges Log**

Keep a small journal or notes app where you track your intuitive nudges throughout the day.
Write them down as soon as they come:

- "Thought of Sarah out of nowhere."
- "Felt like I should take a different road home."

- "Sudden urge to cancel that appointment."

Then, as the day or week unfolds, go back and see what happened. Even if it seems unrelated at the time, you may start to notice patterns or validations. This builds both awareness and trust. The more you track, the more you see how often intuition is guiding you.

**The Mirror Drop-In**

This is a quiet, powerful practice for hearing your soul. Stand or sit in front of a mirror. Soften your gaze. Breathe. Then, ask:

"What do I need to know today?"
Let your mind quiet and see what rises. A word. A feeling. A sentence.
Mirror work can feel intense at first, but it connects you to a deeper part of yourself, and that is where true intuition lives.

**The CLEAR Method**

*A Simple Process to Strengthen Your Intuition*

By now, you've seen that intuition doesn't shout. It speaks in subtleties, sensations, whispers, quiet knowings. And while intuition is natural, it doesn't always feel easy to trust, especially in the beginning.

So, how do you build trust in those moments when life moves fast and you're unsure?

Here's a simple, repeatable process you can use in everyday decisions, big or small. It's what I call the CLEAR Method. Like the AWARE method, each letter represents a step.

**C – Calm**
Pause and breathe. Still your nervous system. You can't hear your inner guidance over the noise of urgency or panic. Come back to your body and take three slow breaths.

**L – Listen**
Tune into your body and inner guidance. Notice what sensations arise. What subtle signals or nudges are present? Intuition often speaks through the body before the mind catches up.

**E – Enquire**
Ask your intuition or higher self. Pose a question, silently or out loud. Keep it simple and open-ended.
"What would be most aligned right now?" or "What do I need to know?" Then let the answer come, without forcing it.

**A – Act**
Take aligned action. It doesn't have to be dramatic. Even small steps, taken with trust, reinforce the connection to your intuition. Action affirms your willingness to listen.

**R – Reflect**

Look back and learn from the outcome. Did the choice feel expansive or constrictive? Did the situation unfold with ease or resistance? Reflection builds discernment.

**Putting the CLEAR Method Into Practice**

Let's say you receive a last-minute invitation to an event. It sounds exciting, but something about it makes you hesitate. You can't tell if it's just resistance or your intuition nudging you to say no. This is the perfect moment to use the CLEAR Method.

**C – Calm**

You pause for a moment, close your eyes, and take three slow breaths, coming into the present moment.

**L – Listen**

You bring your attention inward. You notice your body feels a bit tight in the chest. There's a heaviness, not anxiety, but a quiet discomfort. It's subtle, but it's there. You also notice that your energy feels low and you're craving stillness, not stimulation.

**E – Enquire**

You ask silently: "What would be most aligned for me right now?"
A quiet thought surfaces: *You need rest.* You feel a wave of

relief at the thought of staying home and having a quiet evening to recharge.

**A – Act**
You trust the message. You politely decline the invitation and make a plan to run a bath, journal, and go to bed early.

**R – Reflect**
Later that night, as you're unwinding peacefully, you notice how good it feels to have honoured your energy. You're not feeling FOMO. You're feeling aligned. And in that moment, your trust in your intuition grows stronger.

This is the kind of everyday situation in which intuition speaks, not in dramatic lightning bolts but in small, significant whispers. The more often you go through this process, the more natural it becomes to live intuitively, even when life is loud.

**Let It Be a Practice, not a Performance.**

Remember, this is not about perfection. It is about presence. You are not trying to get every answer right. You are learning to pause, to listen, and to respond from a deeper place within yourself.

Each time you calm your nervous system, listen inwardly, inquire with openness, take aligned action, and reflect on what you discover, you reinforce trust in your intuitive voice. You create new patterns, both spiritually and neurologically, that say, *"I am safe to follow my inner knowing."*

Some days, the guidance will feel strong and obvious. Other days, it might be softer or hidden beneath layers of thought and emotion. That's okay. Keep showing up. Keep practising. Intuition builds over time, not through pressure, but through patience.

Your soul is always speaking. All it asks is that you learn to be still enough to hear.

**In This Chapter, We Explored…**

• How intuition speaks through subtle cues, not logic or volume.
• The 4-step intuition cycle: Receive, Acknowledge, Act, and Celebrate.
• Why this cycle rewires the brain and builds lasting trust in your inner guidance.
• The Traffic Light Game and how it builds intuitive muscle in real time.
• Practical tools like the One-Second Rule, Body Scan, Mirror Drop-In, and more.
• The CLEAR Method, a simple process to calm your system and receive aligned guidance.
• How to turn intuition into a daily practice, not a performance.

## CHAPTER 6

## AWARENESS IN SELF AND SPIRITUAL DEVELOPMENT

> *"With awareness, we are not trapped in our thoughts. We can choose which ones to believe, which ones to follow, and which ones to let go."*
> *-Tara Brach*

Let's be honest, this journey isn't always sunshine and roses. Growth, whether it's personal or spiritual, can be hard. Even when you've learned the tools and mastered the techniques, there are still days when it feels like everything is falling apart. And it becomes even harder if you haven't yet dialled in your two most important spirit senses, awareness and intuition. Because without awareness, self-development becomes a surface-level pursuit. And without intuition, spiritual growth becomes directionless. You're flying blind.

There's a big difference between self-development with awareness and self-development without it. You can read all the books, listen to the podcasts, and do the journaling... but if you're unaware of your patterns, sabotaging behaviours, or the voice of your intuition, then real transformation stays out of reach.

And let's face it, even with awareness, we're still human. We still stumble. We still sabotage. Sometimes, I can see myself falling into an old pattern, and I know what I should be doing, but I don't have it in me that day. I don't feel the drive to push through. I'm tired. Tired of always showing up, always being "on," always being the strong one. Some days, I don't want to be the best version of myself. I just want to rest. I want someone else to carry the load for a change. That's real, too.

This is where awareness is so powerful, not because it makes everything perfect, but because it helps you see. It allows you to witness your patterns, your thoughts, your cycles, even when you're in the thick of them. And that witnessing, that recognition, is what begins to shift things. You may not always act on it in the moment, but awareness means you're no longer asleep to it. You're no longer living unconsciously.

The journey of self-development focuses on improving your mindset, habits, and emotional resilience. It's about becoming more confident, more productive, more capable, often in ways that impact your career, your relationships, and your sense of fulfilment. It's grounded in psychology and science, and for many people, it's the starting point.

But spiritual development invites something deeper. It's about expanding consciousness, awakening to your soul's purpose, and connecting to something greater than yourself, whether that's Source, the Universe, or your higher self. It draws from ancient wisdom and spiritual teachings, guiding you toward inner peace, alignment, and true clarity. And it doesn't happen in isolation. It happens in life, in the challenging moments, in the resistance, in the quiet whispers of your intuition that tell you to go left when the world says go right.

Here's the truth: your growth is limited by your awareness, and your progress depends on your intuition. Without activating these spiritual senses, both your personal and spiritual development reach a ceiling. But once you start cultivating them, everything shifts. You move through life more mindfully. You respond rather than react. You see clearly, even when things are messy. And you stop chasing perfection; instead, you become fully present.

That's where real transformation begins, not in doing more, but in *seeing* more.

**The Missing Link in Mindset Work: Why Awareness Changes Everything (Even Your Brain)**
There's no shortage of mindset tools out there. Affirmations,

journaling prompts, vision boards, morning routines, they're everywhere. And while these tools can be helpful, they're often handed out like spiritual prescriptions without any real depth or discernment. The truth is, most mindset work only scratches the surface, and that surface-level approach can do more harm than good when it's not grounded in awareness.

Let's take affirmations as an example. Repeating "I am happy" when you're not actually happy doesn't magically make you feel better, it creates a disconnect between what you're saying and what you're experiencing. If you keep doing that without acknowledging the gap, your subconscious will label it a lie and reject it. It may dig its heels in even more deeply, reinforcing the very unhappiness you were trying to shift.

But with awareness, affirmations become diagnostic tools. You begin to notice where they *don't* land, and instead of forcing yourself to repeat something that feels fake, you ask, *Why does this feel untrue?* That question opens the door to transformation. You might replace "I am happy" with "I choose to create small moments of happiness," which feels honest, possible, and aligned with where you are now. That's when real rewiring begins, because you're not pushing a lie; you're gently shifting your perspective.

This is the difference that most coaches miss: they teach you to overwrite your thoughts, but instead, we should be paying attention to them. It is important to understand where they come from, why they feel true, and how to choose something new that still honours your current experience. Without awareness, mindset work becomes a spiritual bypass. With awareness, it becomes a roadmap home.

## Your Brain Is Wired for Proof: Enter the RAS

There's a reason this shift in approach works, and it's not just energetic; it's neurological.

At the base of your brainstem sits a cluster of nerves called the **Reticular Activating System** (RAS). Think of it like the bouncer at the door of your mind. Its job is to decide what information gets let in and what gets filtered out. And how does it make that decision? By listening to what *you* repeatedly focus on.

The RAS constantly scans your environment for proof of what you believe, expect, or fear. So, if you believe people can't be trusted, your RAS will highlight every betrayal, snide comment, and subtle rejection, while filtering out the love and support that doesn't match your mental script. If you're constantly focused on lack, your RAS will bring your attention to bills, debt, and everything you *don't* have, while blocking out opportunities that might bring in more.

To put it in simpler terms: your brain finds what you tell it to look for.

A classic example is when you decide you want to buy a red car. Suddenly, red cars are *everywhere.* Did the world suddenly flood with red hatchbacks? No. Your RAS just got the message that red cars are relevant, so now it's pointing them out to you.

The same thing happens with your thoughts. When you tell your brain "Life is hard" or "I never get what I want," the RAS gets to work confirming that story. But when you start to shift your internal dialogue, especially with awareness, the RAS begins to tune into a new reality. One where ease, support, or possibility actually start to exist.

**When I Rewired My Mind and My Life**

You already know my story. Earlier I shared how close I came to ending it all, how the weight of depression, hopelessness, and pain pulled me into the darkest night of my soul. While I didn't have all the words for it back then, what saved me wasn't a miracle cure or a perfect affirmation; it was the power of awareness.

It started with a flicker of thought, not even hope, but *curiosity.* And from that tiny spark, I began to notice what I was focusing on. I started retraining my mind not to default to the pain, but to consider something else. That shift, that new signal to my RAS, began to change what I saw. And that changed everything.

This is why I'm so passionate about teaching awareness first. Because I know what it means to live without it, and I know how powerful life becomes when you finally switch it back on.

The mind is powerful, but it's also programmable. And if you're not choosing what's being programmed, you're living according to old scripts and unconscious patterns. The good news is, the moment you turn on awareness, you start rewriting the code.

So, if you've ever felt like mindset work doesn't "stick," or tools like affirmations feel fake, it's not because you're doing it wrong, it's because you're doing it without *you*. Without the part of you that sees, senses, questions, and chooses. That's awareness. And it's the key to making everything else finally work.

**The Spiral of Awareness: How It Shortens Your Time in the Dark**

Healing isn't linear. No matter what the self-help books or polished Instagram quotes say, real transformation looks more like a spiral than a straight line. Life brings us lessons in themes, patterns that return again and again, each time in a slightly different form, often disguised, but always familiar. They show up in your relationships, your finances, your sense of worth, your health, and your fears. At first, you don't notice the pattern. You're just trying to survive it.

In the early stages of your journey, you're running blind through these cycles. The pain hits hard, confusion reigns, and it can take months or even years to understand what really happened, if you ever get to that point at all. But the more you cultivate awareness, the more you begin to see. You start noticing the signs earlier. You recognize the feeling in your body, the narrative in your mind, the subtle energetic shift that tells you: *Ah, this again.*

This is where awareness becomes your superpower.

Over time, as your awareness sharpens, the timeline between *impact* and *insight* shortens. What used to take you a year to process now takes six months. What once spiralled you for weeks might now only take a few days to move through. And eventually, you'll find yourself in a moment of emotional charge, able to stop, take a breath, and name it: *This is that old story again. I see it. I know it. I choose differently now.*

This is what I mean when I say awareness shortens your time in the dark.

It doesn't mean you won't revisit old wounds. You will. The themes of your life will keep spiralling around, not to torture you, but to offer you deeper mastery, more freedom, more truth. The difference is: with awareness, you're not trapped in the dark anymore. You're walking through it with a torch.

Eventually, you'll be able to meet these moments with such presence and clarity that you shift them in seconds, not months. That kind of power—the ability to meet life as it is, to recognize your patterns without drowning in them—is what turns healing into liberation.

This is the real work, and it prepares us to move into the deeper layers of healing in both self- and spiritual development.

**Healing is a Spiral, not a Straight Line**

You'll circle back to the same wounds sometimes. You'll think you've dealt with something, only for it to rise again in a deeper form. That's not failure, that's healing.

Every time you return, you meet yourself with more wisdom, more compassion, and more clarity. That's what changes everything.

So, if you're in the middle of your own journey, whether it's about weight, worth, or anything else, trust the layers. Let your awareness guide you. Let your intuition speak. And know that every step, even the painful ones, is leading you back to your true self.

**Introducing the A.I. Code: Awareness and Intuition as Your Spirit Technology**

Until now, we've discussed awareness and intuition as separate concepts, but what I've realised over the years is that these two spirit senses don't just work alongside your growth... they are the foundation of it.

Together, they form what I call **The A.I. Code**, a personal operating system that, once activated, upgrades every other part of your life. It's not artificial intelligence. It's your inner intelligence, **Awareness and Intuition**.

I use the word "code" intentionally. Because just like lines of code tell a computer what to do, your internal code — the beliefs you hold, the patterns you follow, and the signals you respond to — guides how you experience your life.

But here's the thing: most people are running on outdated code—scripts they didn't choose, programs inherited from trauma, culture, family, and fear. They're operating from conditioning, not consciousness.

That's why I created the A.I. Code, not as a method but as a movement. A return to the original technology which equips every soul with the ability to *see* (awareness) and to *sense* (intuition).

These are the missing pieces in most spiritual and personal development practices. You've probably felt it. Like something important was missing, even when you were "doing the work." That's because without awareness and intuition, you're applying powerful tools... with disconnected hands.

Let's break it down.

- **Awareness** is your ability to observe without judgment. It's your inner witness, the part of you that can name what's happening *without* getting lost in it. It shows you your patterns, your default reactions, your mental scripts. It shines a light on what's true.

- **Intuition** is your inner guidance, the voice of your soul. It's not louder than logic, but it's wiser. It doesn't explain, it *knows*. It speaks in nudges, whispers, sensations, and clarity that arrives before thought. It knows what's right for you, even when it doesn't make sense to anyone else.

When you integrate these two together, something shifts.

You stop reacting and start responding.

You stop outsourcing your truth and start trusting yourself.

You stop repeating the past and start creating the future.

That's the A.I. Code in action.

And now, I want to show you how this changes everything. You don't need to throw out the tools you love. You just need to bring *yourself* back into them. When Awareness and Intuition are your starting point, the same tools you've used before become entirely new.

Let me show you what I mean.

## The Tools You Know, Transformed by Awareness and Intuition

There's no shortage of tools in the self and spiritual development space. Journaling. Meditation. Inner child work. Shadow work. Vision boards. Breathwork. Nervous system regulation. The list goes on. These practices are everywhere, and for good reason. They *work*.

But here's what most people don't realise: the effectiveness of these tools depends on the level of **awareness** and **intuition** you bring into them.

Without awareness, you're just going through the motions.

Without intuition, you're following someone else's map instead of your own inner compass.

When you integrate the A.I. Code, when awareness and intuition become your *starting point*, not an afterthought, the tools you've used a hundred times start to work *differently*. Deeper. Truer. More aligned. And they actually begin to create the transformation they promised all along.

Let's explore six of the most commonly used tools and how the A.I. Code changes everything.

### 1. Journaling

**Without A.I. Code:** Journaling often becomes a mental dump, a place to offload feelings, repeat affirmations, or follow templated prompts. You might write "I am enough" every day, but never actually feel it. You're processing, but not necessarily transforming.

**With A.I. Code:** Journaling becomes a conversation with your soul. You use awareness to observe your thought patterns instead of getting lost in them. You listen for intuitive nudges, insights that drop in as whispers, not noise. Questions like "What am I not seeing?" open more than just pages. It opens perception. You begin to *receive* through journaling, not just release.

## 2. Meditation

**Without A.I. Code:** Meditation is often treated like a fix for stress. People try to "quiet the mind" and get frustrated when it doesn't work. It becomes a performance, sitting still, trying not to think, waiting for peace to arrive.

**With A.I. Code:** Meditation becomes a space of *listening* instead of silence. You don't fight your thoughts, you witness them. You notice patterns. You follow your breath not to escape your mind, but to observe it. And when your intuition speaks in images, feelings, or sudden knowing, you're present enough to catch it. You leave your practice not just calm but *connected*.

## 3. Vision Boards

**Without A.I. Code:** Vision boards become a collage of what you *think* you want, often based on societal ideals or comparison. You cut out pictures of dream homes or luxury cars, but they don't light you up. Or worse, they activate shame. You start feeling like you're not enough until those things arrive.

**With A.I. Code:** Your vision board becomes an energetic map of alignment. You use awareness to notice what genuinely excites your body. You tune into your intuitive yes before placing anything on the board. It becomes a visual anchor for what your soul is truly calling you toward, not what the world says you should want. The board starts feeling alive, resonant, and true.

## 4. Shadow Work

**Without A.I. Code:** Shadow work becomes analytical, a dissection of your "dark parts." You make lists of faults or triggers, but stay stuck in the analysis. It can even turn into self-judgment in disguise.

**With A.I. Code:** Shadow work becomes sacred witnessing. You hold your shadow with compassion. Awareness helps you recognise the root, not just the reaction. Intuition shows you what's ready to be healed now, not what your ego wants to fix. It stops being a mental exercise and becomes a deep act of reclamation.

## 5. Nervous System Regulation

**Without A.I. Code:** You apply breathwork, tapping, and other modalities like prescribed techniques. You feel momentary relief, but patterns keep returning. You're managing the symptoms, not the signal.

**With A.I. Code:** You begin with presence. Awareness helps you identify why your body is dysregulated in the first place. You notice your responses without judgment. Intuition guides you to the right tool in the right moment, because not every situation calls for stillness. Sometimes it calls for sound. For movement. For softness. You regulate not just to cope, but to *connect* with yourself.

## 6. Affirmations

**Without A.I. Code:** Affirmations are used to overwrite negativity, but if they don't feel true, your subconscious resists them. You repeat "I am abundant" while your body tightens. Your mind calls it a lie.

**With A.I. Code:** Affirmations become mirrors, not scripts. You use awareness to feel into what lands and what doesn't. You adjust your language with intuition. "I am abundant" becomes "I'm learning to receive abundance in new ways." That subtle shift aligns truth and intention, and the affirmation starts planting seeds instead of sparking resistance. It feels *possible*. And that's where transformation begins.

Your tools probably aren't the problem; it's how you're using them. They don't need replacing. They need *rewiring* through the lens of awareness and intuition. The power has always been there. What's often been missing is *you*, the deeper, wiser part of you that sees clearly and knows what's true. When that part is present, everything changes. That's the shift the A.I. Code brings.

**When You're Triggered: The Moment Awareness Matters Most**

Let's talk about something real, the part of this journey that doesn't look pretty on paper.

You're scrolling social media, and someone's post makes your blood boil.
Your partner says something innocent, but it hits like a punch. You watch someone succeed and feel an ache in your chest that you can't explain.

That's a trigger or as I like to call them, ACTIVATIONS.

And as much as we'd all love to rise above it, triggers are part of the work. They're one of the most *important* parts, if you know how to work with them.

When you're triggered/activated, your nervous system lights up. Old beliefs flare. You go into defence mode, fight, flight, freeze, or fawn. Your brain pulls from past experiences to try and protect you, and your perception narrows to match that threat.

But here's what most people miss: *a trigger isn't just a reaction, it's an activation from your soul.*

It's your body trying to show you where something still hurts. Where something still feels unsafe, unseen, or unhealed.

This is where the A.I. Code becomes your anchor.

- **Awareness** lets you pause. Instead of being swept away by the emotion or making someone else wrong, you name what's happening: *"I'm activated. Something in me just got touched."*
- **Intuition** helps you go deeper. It guides you to ask the right questions, not from your head, but from your soul:
*What does this remind me of?*
*Where have I felt this before?*
*What is this trying to teach me about myself?*

When you meet a trigger with awareness and intuition, it no longer becomes something to suppress or spiral into, it becomes a moment of truth. A doorway. A turning point.

And not every trigger needs to be "healed" in the moment. Sometimes the most powerful thing you can do is *witness it without judgment*. To simply say: *"Oh... there you are."* That alone shifts the energy. It's like the monster in the closet. At first you're afraid of it, but as you become more aware of it, it loses power over you.

The more you practice this, the faster your system learns that you are safe. You start to see patterns more clearly. You learn to trust your responses. You begin to understand yourself and others at a deeper level.

You can't bypass your way to freedom.
You can't affirm your way out of trauma.
You can't manifest your way around a wound you refuse to look at.

But you *can* become so aware that you stop being ruled by your reactions.
You *can* become so attuned that your triggers become teachers.
You *can* become so deeply connected to your intuition that even your most uncomfortable moments start pointing you home.

This is what makes the A.I. Code not just a framework but a lifeline, especially in the moments when you feel most human.

So, if you've ever thought, *"I should be further along than this,"* or *"Why am I still getting triggered by this stuff?"*, take a breath.

You're not broken. You're being shown something.
And what you do with that insight… that's what transforms everything.

Because that's the real power of awareness, it doesn't just help you heal. It helps you *integrate*. Every trigger, every spiral, every hard-earned lesson becomes part of a greater unfolding.

And that unfolding? It's not random. It's pointing you toward your purpose.

Life purpose is one of those big, looming questions, but it's not as far away as it seems. I've included it here because what most people don't realise is this: your life has already been shaping you for it. If we look back with awareness, we start to see patterns, threads, and moments of truth we once overlooked. Purpose isn't something you have to chase. It's something you uncover, often hiding in plain sight, woven through your own story.

**Finding Your Soul Purpose**

One of the most common questions in the self-development space is, *"What is my purpose?"*

As we begin to awaken to the realisation that life holds more than we've been led to believe, something within us shifts. It's as if a switch is flicked inside, a quiet but powerful nudge that calls us to seek more meaning, more fulfilment, more truth.

We start yearning not just to be happier or more content, but to grow. To evolve. To contribute.
Our focus moves from what we can *get* to how we can *serve*.

We begin to realise that each of us carries a unique gift, something deeply personal and profoundly needed in the world.

I believe every person has a **life theme**, a thread woven through their experiences that reveals their purpose. This theme is not random. It's shaped by our stories, our traumas, and the moments that challenged us most.

The difficult chapters of your life were not just painful; they were formative. They offered opportunities to develop strengths, gifts, and inner wisdom that might have otherwise remained dormant.

**Pain Becomes Purpose**

For instance, someone who grew up in a household with alcoholic or abusive parents may have learned, out of necessity, to read subtle shifts in body language or energy to stay safe.

While that experience may have been heartbreaking, it also forged a powerful skill, one that could later become a profound gift. That same person might go on to become a leading expert in body language, a gifted coach, a compassionate therapist, or even a world-class detective. What once felt like a survival mechanism becomes a superpower when awareness is brought to it. Our pain, when acknowledged and transformed, becomes purpose. And through that purpose, we begin to understand *why* we are here.

**Purpose Isn't a Job Title**

Before we explore how to uncover your purpose, I want to make one thing clear: there is no single path or formula to discovering why you are here.

Your purpose isn't confined to a job title or a role society deems worthy.
There are a million different ways to serve, and your soul's purpose may express itself in ways you've never imagined.

You might feel deeply called to help others, but that doesn't automatically mean you need to become a doctor or a therapist.

You could be a teacher, a writer, a coach, or someone who creates beautiful art that inspires and heals.

The mistake many people make is believing that purpose has to look a certain way.
We get caught in societal expectations and forget that our purpose isn't about fitting into a box; it's about becoming who we truly are.

*True purpose is found where your passions, natural gifts, and life experiences intersect.*

It's what lights you up.
It's what makes you come alive.

As I walk you through my own timeline below, I hope it helps you see how the seemingly random or painful moments in your life may have been pointing you toward your purpose all along.

**Look for the Clues**

One powerful clue to discovering your purpose lies in what naturally draws your attention.

Someone once said, *"If you want to find your purpose, look at your bookshelf."*
The books you're drawn to… the topics you keep returning to all hold clues.

My bookshelf clearly mirrors my life theme: spirituality, healing, psychology, books on body language, statement analysis, intuition, awareness, and more.
It's no coincidence.

**The Timeline of My Life (Exercise)**

Now, I'd like to guide you through a powerful exercise I use with my clients and students.
It's called the **Timeline of My Life**, designed to help you uncover the themes that have shaped you and may ultimately lead you to your purpose.

But there's more.

This exercise is also incredibly helpful for healing.
By mapping out your life, you may begin to recognise old wounds, limiting beliefs, and unresolved patterns asking to be seen and transformed.

**How to Begin:**

- Take several sheets of paper and tape them together to form one long piece, or use a whiteboard if you prefer.
- Start at birth and begin creating a timeline of your life.
- This is not something you have to do in one sitting; it's a process.
- Keep it somewhere visible, and as memories surface over the next few days or weeks, jot them down.

Write *everything*, big and small, joyful and painful.
These moments are puzzle pieces.
Some will show you your gifts.
Others will show you what needs healing.

On the next page is an example of my own timeline.

# SPIRITUAL A.I.

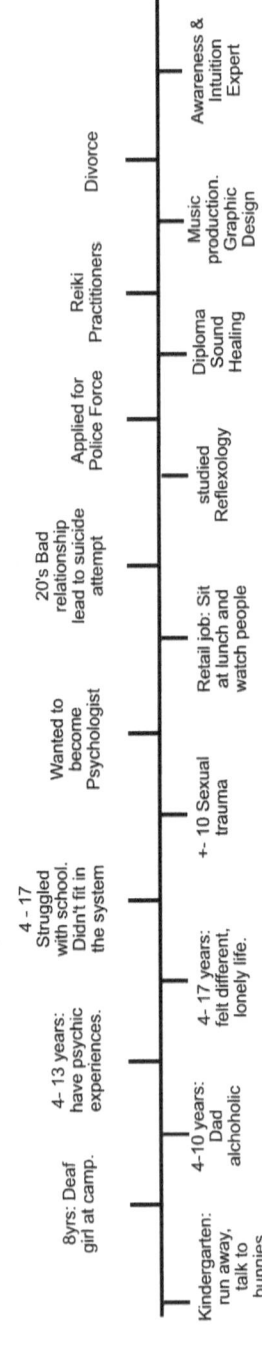

Here's a rough outline of my own life to show you how this process works, and how clearly your life's theme begins to emerge when you look at it through the lens of awareness and curiosity.

From an early age, I didn't fit into the structure of the schooling system. My mom tells a story of me packing my little suitcase and marching myself out of kindergarten because I wasn't happy there. Even at that age, I rejected being forced into a box. I was different, and I knew it.

There was also a story published in our local newspapaer of which my mom still has the newspaper clipping about how I would talk to the bunnies at kindergarten.
Sweet and innocent, that moment was also the first public sign of my intuitive connection.
I didn't just talk, I *communicated.*

When I was around eight, we went camping, and I met a girl on a trampoline. When I tried to talk to her, her father explained she was deaf. Something stirred in me. I felt her loneliness, and I immediately wanted to learn sign language so I could connect with her.

That moment awakened my desire to help others feel seen, heard, and less alone.

Between the ages of 4 and 13, I had many "spooky" experiences, energetic presences, footsteps behind me, a knowing that couldn't be explained. But instead of being nurtured, these experiences were dismissed as my imagination. It planted early seeds of doubt around my intuitive gifts. School never felt like a safe space. I was constantly compared to my brother, who excelled academically, and I internalised the belief that I wasn't good enough.

At home, my father's alcoholism and the unpredictable chaos that came with it forced me to become hyper-aware of my environment. I developed a kind of emotional radar, constantly scanning for danger or energy shifts, which became one of my greatest gifts later in life.

After school, I dreamed of becoming a psychologist or a teacher, but my grades weren't high enough, so I started working in retail. I remember sitting on the edge of a fountain at lunchtime, watching people walk past, reading their energy, sensing their emotions.
I didn't know it then, but I was already pursuing my purpose. I had started exploring spirituality and other belief systems, trying to make sense of what I knew to be true deep inside.

I climbed the corporate ladder to become a regional supervisor in merchandising, which led me to the city, and eventually to the relationship that led to the lowest point in my life, which I shared earlier in this book.

In 2005, I got married. In 2006, we moved to Australia, and

from there, the puzzle pieces of my purpose began to fall into place.

Each step felt divinely timed.

I first studied Reflexology, but life had other plans, and in 2010, my second daughter was born. In 2013, feeling a renewed pull to serve, I applied to the police force. I passed every step of the application, but my foot gave way when it came time to run in the fitness part.
It was as if the universe had other plans for me, and it did.

While I was waiting to reapply, I worked in a metaphysical store. During that time, I was guided to sound healing… and, later, Reiki.

Sound healing led me to record my own music, which led me to graphic design so that I could create my own CD-covers.
I developed skills I never thought I'd need, but they all became tools in the bigger picture.

Seeing clients, I realised I had an uncanny ability to help people find their blind spots, their patterns, blocks, and limiting beliefs. I could see what others couldn't. Every single experience I had ever lived had prepared me for this.

Today, I am a Transformational Coach, a Spiritual Teacher, and a Healer. I'm the host of *The Spiritual AI Podcast,* a published author, and a guide.  I live in alignment with who I was always meant to be, and I use every single skill and scar to serve others on their journey.

On the next page, I have highlighted what these moments in my life did for me on this journey.

# The Authentic Intelligence

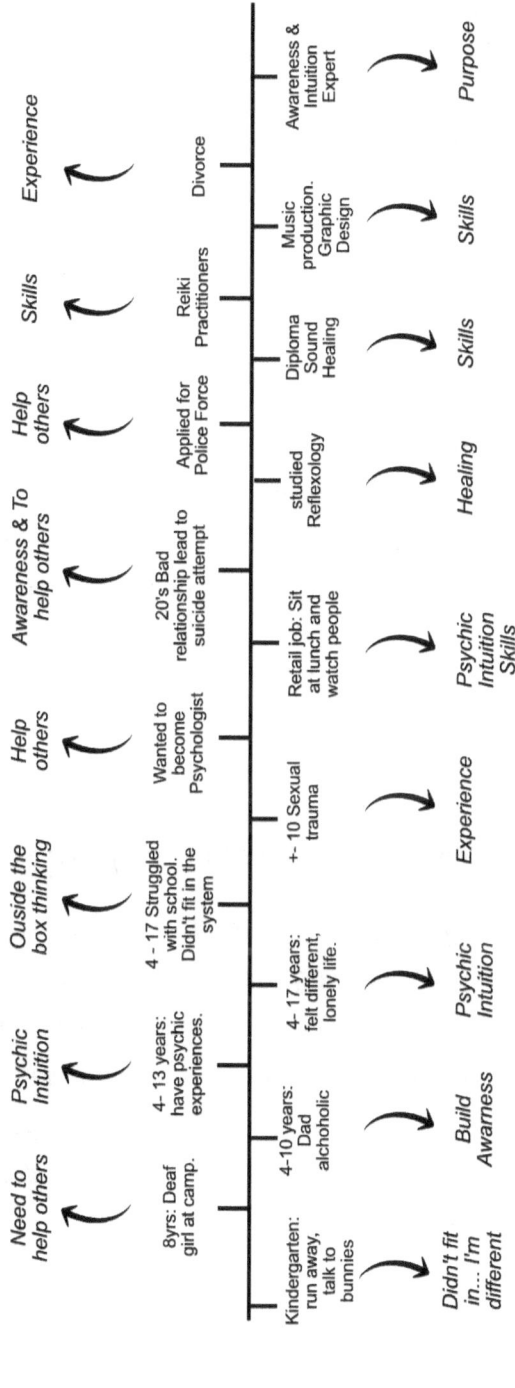

**Your Purpose Lives Within You**

Looking back on my timeline, it's so clear.

From childhood, I was always connected to something deeper. I was always meant to help others in whatever way I could.

And now, through awareness and intuition, I help people find clarity, ease, and purpose.
I help them remember their own power.

Purpose isn't just about a career.
It's about coming home to yourself.
It's about living in alignment with who you truly are, and doing what lights you up, so you can become the person the world needs most.


**One Piece of Wisdom**

I heard something recently that struck me deeply. A man said:

*"It's a dangerous thing to discover your purpose. Because when you discover your purpose, you become an irritation to people. You'll upset people. When you discover your purpose, you declare your independence because you'll no longer let others dictate who you should be. When you find your purpose, food will become a stumbling block, and sleep will become a hindrance. Purpose prolongs life."*

That is the truth.
And that's also why we're conditioned away from it.

We're trained to ask permission, to follow the rules, to ignore our intuition.
We're told to colour inside the lines, stick to the plan, get the job, pay the debt, and keep our heads down.

Because if we ever stopped to listen to the voice inside, the one that *knows*, we'd become impossible to control.

When you discover your purpose, *you free yourself.*
And when enough people do that... we change the world.

**Carol's Story** *(name changed)*

I want to share a story from one of my coaching clients, Carol, because her journey is a perfect example of how your purpose doesn't always have to be your profession.

Like many people, Carol reached a point in her life where she felt a quiet inner nudge. She loved her job, but something inside her kept asking, "What's my purpose?" She described herself as a healer at heart, but as a bookkeeper, she spent most of her day staring at spreadsheets and numbers, not exactly what you'd call a healing space.

In one of our coaching sessions, she said, *"I honestly love working with numbers. I'm good at it. I can't imagine doing anything else... but I still feel like something's missing."*

So, we dug a little deeper. I asked her what people often come to her for, outside of her job. She paused, smiled, and said, *"Advice. People are always coming to me for advice, friends, family"*, even clients of the business she was working for. *"I don't always have the answers but know how to listen."*

And there it was.

The purpose wasn't missing. She'd just been imagining her purpose had to look a certain way.

But purpose doesn't always mean changing careers or walking away from what you've built. Sometimes, it's simply about recognising who you *already are*, and owning the ways your gifts are already being expressed.

Carol didn't need to quit her job to live her purpose. She just needed to see that her ability to bring calm, clarity, and insight to those around her was already *part* of her purpose, and it had been there all along.

If you've ever felt like you don't know what your purpose is, or you're unsure how it fits into your current life, these reflection questions might help bring clarity. Sometimes the answers are right there, woven into who you've always been.

**Reflection Questions**
If you find yourself unsure about what you're genuinely passionate about, or you're struggling to identify how your

purpose could take shape, these questions might help point you in the right direction. They can also offer insight into your natural strengths and even how you could shape those into a business or calling.

- What do people often thank you for?
- What kind of advice do others naturally seek from you?
- What do people consistently come to you for?
- Are there issues in the world that deeply frustrate you or tug at your heart?
- What personal challenges have you already overcome?
- What transformation have you gone through that you could now guide someone else through?

These questions are powerful clues.
They help reveal what comes naturally to you, the gifts you might be overlooking because they're so integrated into who you are.

Now it's your turn.
Let your timeline reveal the theme of your life.
Let it show you the pain, yes, *but also the brilliance.*

**Head's Up:**
Purpose work often opens the door to healing. When we start living in alignment, everything that's not aligned begins to rise to the surface—the wounds, the beliefs, the patterns. That's why awareness and intuition aren't just useful; they're

essential. They become your torch as you walk through the layers of yourself.

## There's a Real Danger to NOT Being Connected to Your Inner Guidance

We don't talk about this enough in the self and spiritual development space, but we need to.

While healing and growth work is deeply powerful, it can also be deeply damaging if it's not grounded in the right foundation.

If you dive into shadow work or breathwork, for instance, without a strong sense of awareness and intuitive connection, you can unknowingly open up deep trauma that you're not equipped to process. You might unearth memories or emotions that leave you feeling heavy, disoriented, or worse, re-traumatised. You can get pulled back into the very darkness you came to heal.

When you approach healing, spiritual work, or self-development without a stable connection to yourself and your own inner guidance system, you end up mimicking what others are doing. You reach for tools that might not be right for you. You override your own signals, forcing yourself to "heal," "manifest," or "elevate" when your nervous system is actually begging you to pause, to grieve, or simply to be.

Without awareness and intuition, this work doesn't just fall short, it can actually deepen the very patterns you came here to change.

It can re-traumatise.
It can reinforce old programming.
It can make you believe *you're the problem* when really, you were just missing the connection.

And that's not even touching on the psychic and energetic impact of being in a room with 50 other people releasing emotional baggage, without the inner filters to manage what's yours and what isn't. That level of unconscious exposure can leave you more cracked open than empowered.

This is why I'm so passionate about leading with awareness and intuition.
They're not extras. They're not nice-to-haves. They are the *essentials*.

Think of it this way: **awareness is the bowl**, and **intuition is the spoon**.

Breath work, shadow work, nervous system regulation, and affirmations are the ingredients to bake the cake, but without a container to hold this all, you can't bake your cake. You're left with a mess of disconnected parts if you don't have a bowl to keep it all together and a spoon to stir and activate it. It's wishful thinking to think you can do the healing work without awareness and intuition. You're trying to do deep, nourishing work with no container and no way to actually receive it.

Without awareness, you manifest and grow from your subconscious programming, not your true potential. You repeat patterns. You think you're evolving, but you're still operating from fear, people-pleasing, scarcity, or unhealed wounds. Awareness gives you space. It lets you see clearly. It helps you understand what's really driving your decisions so you can reclaim your power of choice. Because you can't create a new reality if you're unaware of the one you're still unconsciously living in and without intuition, you end up following someone else's blueprint. You chase step-by-step methods that weren't meant for you. You push yourself to keep going when your soul is asking you to pivot or pause. Intuition is your original GPS. It tells you when to act, when to wait, and when something isn't aligned, even if your friend said it's amazing for them. It might not be for you.

Together, awareness and intuition don't just support your healing.
They protect it.
They guide it.
They *anchor* it.

When those two spirit senses are switched on, your healing becomes personal, your growth becomes embodied, and your path finally starts to make sense.

And that's the moment the work starts to *truly* work.
That's the moment you come back to yourself.

**In This Chapter, We Explored...**

• How awareness and intuition are not just supportive tools, but the spiritual senses that *must* come first if you want true transformation, in both personal and spiritual development.

• The difference between surface-level and embodied growth, and how the A.I. Code helps you move from doing the work to *becoming* the work.

• Why common practices like journaling, meditation, and shadow work often fall flat (or even cause harm) without a strong foundation of awareness and intuition.

• How triggers, patterns, and emotional spirals aren't signs of failure, but powerful invitations, and how awareness helps you navigate them with clarity instead of fear.

• The real risks of skipping these foundational senses, including spiritual bypassing, reinforcing old programming, or re-traumatising yourself in the name of "healing."

• The truth about purpose: that it's not something you have to chase, but something you uncover, often hidden in the threads of your own life story.

## CHAPTER 7

## AWARENESS IN HEALING

> *"Awareness doesn't get rid of your pain, it gives you the space to meet it with compassion and choose differently."*
> *-Unknown*

**The Body-Mind Connection and the Truth Beneath the Weight**

Most people think healing is a straight line- you identify the problem, fix it, and move on. But healing doesn't work that way. Transformation isn't a one-time epiphany or a clean cut from the past. It's an unravelling. A remembering. A peeling back of layers, each one revealing more of the truth that has always been there.

Let me share something close to home to show you what that means. This is how the spiral of healing revealed itself in one of the most personal parts of my journey, my relationship with my body and weight.

## The Innocent Beginning

As a child, I was naturally skinny. I never thought twice about food or how I looked. I ran, played, and lived in a body that felt like mine. There was no shame. No control. Just being.

This is where we all start, in a state of innocence and connection with ourselves, before the world begins to whisper its expectations into our ears.

But somewhere along the way, something changed.

## The Moment of Programming

I still remember the moment. I was young, maybe around ten or eleven. I was sad because I didn't have a boyfriend. My dad asked me why I looked so sad, and I told him. That's when my dad said something that stuck with me like glue:

"Pretty girls don't get boys. Boys think they're already taken."

Looking back now, I can understand what he was saying, but in that moment, I heard that I was pretty and that I wouldn't be able to get a boyfriend. Something inside me shifted. My young mind subconsciously decided: *Then I won't be pretty.*

And so, I started eating.

Not because I was hungry. Not because I loved food. But because some part of me believed that being attractive would mean that I would be single forever. And being alone is another deep fear I used to carried.

## The Battle on the Surface

As a young adult, I struggled constantly with my weight. I tried everything: diet pills, restrictive eating, punishments, willpower. And for a while, some of it worked. I'd lose the weight, feel a moment of pride… and then gain it all back.

Over and over again.

It was exhausting. I kept trying to change what I saw in the mirror without understanding why it was there in the first place. I thought the weight was the problem. But it wasn't. It was just a symptom, a messenger, really, asking me to look deeper.

At the time, I didn't know how.

## The First Layer of Awareness

Years later, in the middle of some deep inner work, that memory of my dad's comment resurfaced. I connected the dots. I saw how that one sentence had shaped my relationship with my body for decades.

It was like the lights came on in a dark room.

I remember thinking: *That's it. That's why I've held onto this weight.*

It was powerful—liberating, even. But here's the part people don't tell you: Even that realisation didn't change my eating habits.

Why? Because there were still more layers.

> *"Your body is not a problem to solve;*
> *it's a story to listen to."*
> *– Unknown*

**The Deeper Layer: Trauma in the Body**

Sometime later, I was listening to a podcast, one of those soul-stirring, truth-hitting kinds, when another layer peeled back.

The host was talking about how many women carry weight around their stomachs as a form of protection after sexual trauma or unwanted attention. It hit me hard. I had never connected my weight to that part of my story.

But when I stopped and really felt into it, I knew. I had experienced multiple sexual encounters throughout my life that, whether I labelled them as trauma or not, had left deep imprints on my body.

And suddenly, my body made perfect sense.

The weight wasn't just a physical thing. It was emotional. Energetic. My belly had become an armour, a sacred space holding years of stories, pain, shame, and a deep desire to feel safe.

This was a different level of awareness, a new level of truth. And I knew in my bones that *this would be the real work.*

**The Path to Integration**

From that moment forward, my journey began to shift. I stopped trying to "fix" my body and started listening to it. I walked and moved, not to punish myself, but to be with myself. I gave love to the parts I once resented. I honoured the version of me that had always been trying to protect me, even through the weight, even through the withdrawal, even through the pain.

Healing isn't fast. It isn't linear. But it is real.

And this is what I've learned: true transformation happens in layers. What starts as a desire to lose weight or feel better on the outside nearly always leads inward, into old beliefs, buried memories, emotional patterns, and energetic imprints.

And that's where awareness and intuition come in—not as tips or techniques but as sacred senses, inner compasses that help you see beyond the surface and into the truth of who you really are.

## Listening to the Body as a Messenger

Your body is always talking to you. Whether through pain, fatigue, cravings, skin breakouts, or subtle tension, it communicates in the only language it knows: sensation.

But most of us were never taught how to listen. We've been conditioned to override discomfort, suppress symptoms, and push through pain. We use medication to numb, distractions to avoid, and affirmations to talk over what the body is trying to say. But real healing begins when we bring awareness to the conversation our body is trying to have with us.

When you stop seeing symptoms as problems and start treating them as messages, you enter into a relationship with your body instead of a battle.

Let me share a simple example from my own life. When I eat too much sugar, my feet start to hurt. It's consistent. It's not dramatic. But it's clear. That pain is my body's way of saying, "Something isn't working." Before I developed this level of awareness, I would have ignored it, or worse, reached for more sugar to cope with feeling off.

Now I pause. I notice. I ask:
"What are you trying to tell me?"

That's the difference awareness makes. It doesn't always mean you get it right the first time. It just means you're listening.

You're paying attention. You're open to learning the language of your own body.

**What If Nothing's "Wrong"?**

Sometimes the body's signals are less about illness and more about the energies behind it.

Tightness in your chest after a phone call might not mean you're sick; it might mean you're out of integrity in that relationship. A sore throat might not just be a virus; it might be the result of things left unsaid. A sluggish gut might be connected to something you've emotionally resisted "digesting."

This is where awareness becomes more than mindfulness; it becomes a healing tool. It allows you to feel, observe, and reflect before reacting or suppressing.

**The Body Remembers**

In *The Body Keeps the Score*, trauma expert Bessel van der Kolk writes:

*"The body keeps the score: if the memory of trauma is encoded in the viscera, in heartbreaking and gut-wrenching emotions, then it needs to be accessed and processed through the body."*

This quote changed the way I viewed healing.

It validated what I had already come to know through my own journey: that symptoms are more than physical, they are somatic memories. Your body holds onto what your conscious mind has long forgotten or buried. And awareness is how we begin to gently unravel it.

**Translating the Body's Language**

Your body is wise, but it doesn't speak English. It speaks of sensation, tension, tightness, and symptoms. Funny enough, your subconscious does try to translate this, often through the language we use every day without realising it.

Think about the expressions we casually say:

- "That made me sick to my stomach."
- "I'm carrying so much on my shoulders."
- "I need to get this off my chest."
- "They're a pain in my neck."
- "That situation's hard to swallow."

These aren't just metaphors. They are intuitive translations of what your body is feeling. They give you insight into the underlying emotion or energetic pattern that might be manifesting physically.

By bringing awareness to these phrases, you can start to decode what your body is trying to tell you, especially when you're dealing with ongoing or unexplained discomfort.

**Here are 20 common expressions and the body clues they may reveal:**

- "Pain in the neck" - Feeling annoyed or burdened by someone/something
- "Carrying the weight of the world"- Overwhelm, too much responsibility
- "Gut feeling" - Intuitive knowing, trust/distrust issues
- "Sick to my stomach" - Deep discomfort, rejection, dread
- "Heartbroken" - Deep emotional loss or grief
- "Can't stomach it" - Emotional rejection, unwillingness to accept something
- "Get this off my chest" - Needing to express truth, holding unspoken emotions
- "Tied up in knots" - Anxiety, confusion, fear
- "Cold feet" - Fear of commitment or moving forward
- "Head spinning" - Overthinking, overwhelm, too much input
- "Lost my voice" - Not speaking the truth, feeling silenced
- "Shouldering a burden" - Taking on others' problems or emotional loads
- "Got under my skin" - Irritation, something that's really bothering you

- "Backstabbed" - Betrayal, loss of trust
- "Butterflies in my stomach" - Excitement, nervous anticipation
- "On edge" - High alert, anxious, not feeling safe
- "My back against the wall" - Feeling trapped, no way out
- "It's eating me up inside" - Guilt, resentment, regret
- "Walking on eggshells" - Hyper-vigilance, fear of upsetting someone
- "Broken-hearted" - Emotional wounding, sadness, grief

Once you begin noticing how your language reflects your inner world, you'll see your body not as a stranger, but as a storyteller, always trying to get your attention in the most familiar ways.

You can even start keeping a journal of the phrases you say or hear often. Ask yourself:

- What's going on in my life right now that relates to this phrase?
- Is there a physical sensation or symptom that connects?
- What emotion am I not acknowledging?

This kind of awareness turns vague discomfort into clear communication, and from there, healing can truly begin.

## Awareness Isn't About Fear, It's About Freedom

Awareness doesn't mean becoming hyper-focused on every sensation or symptom. It means becoming more connected to your body's wisdom, more present, more attuned, more empowered.

When you begin to see the link between your choices, your emotions, and how your body feels, you stop feeling helpless. You stop outsourcing your healing. You step into partnership with yourself.

You're not being dramatic. You're paying attention. And when you listen with curiosity instead of fear, your body no longer needs to shout to be heard.

## Don't Claim It: The Power of Language and Mental Framing

Awareness isn't just about noticing what's happening in your body; it's also about paying attention to the words you use to describe it.

I have a rule in my house:
**Don't walk around claiming you're sick.**
Before you think I'm a cold, heartless mother, let me explain.

My daughters know that when they're not feeling well, maybe they're getting a cold or their sinuses are playing up, they absolutely come to me for support. They know to rest, hydrate, and do what's needed to feel better. But one thing they don't do is go around saying, *"I'm sick."*

Instead, they say, *"I'm recovering from…"*

That one simple shift in language makes a big difference. Because words are powerful, they're like agreements. And when you constantly affirm illness, even casually, your body and subconscious mind take it on as truth.

**Words Can Reinforce or Release**

A few years ago, I started to experience pain and stiffness in my shoulder. I remembered my mother had developed bone spurs and needed surgery, so I went to my GP just to check. The scan came back clear, no spurs.

The doctor explained that a lot of women who go through menopause struggle with frozen shoulders. It's just something that happens. She then said, "It usually takes about two years to resolve, and in some cases it requires surgery to gain full function again."

Now here's the difference: I didn't take that as my truth. I heard it, sure. But I immediately said, *"I don't accept that. Mine will heal much faster."*

I didn't ignore the pain. I adapted, asked for help, bought clothes that were easier to put on so that I wouldn't have to feel or think about my shoulder, and honoured what my body needed. But I **NEVER** walked around saying, *"I have a frozen shoulder."*

In fact, over the entire seven months that I dealt with the issue, I probably mentioned it only five times, and even then, I would say, *"I'm recovering from a frozen shoulder."*

Seven months later, I had about 90% of my range of motion back. The remaining 10% returned so gradually I barely noticed it.

**Claiming Language = Claiming Energy**

When you say, *"I have [X],"* you're not just giving information, you're forming identity. The more you repeat it, the more your subconscious embeds it as part of who you are. It becomes harder to release because you've wrapped your energy around it.

This isn't about toxic positivity or denying how you feel. It's about not *owning* something that is meant to move through you.

Awareness means being mindful of the stories you tell, even the quiet ones. Especially the quiet ones.

**Intuition in the Healing Journey**
While awareness helps us notice what's happening in the

moment, intuition gives us access to something even deeper, the knowing beneath the knowing.

Intuition doesn't always follow logic. It won't always give you a full explanation. But when you learn to trust it, it can guide you to solutions you would never have considered, often long before the mind can catch up.

Let me share a powerful experience where my intuition quite literally saved my life.

**When Intuition guides you to Healing.**

Last year, I kept seeing Instagram reels pop up about parasite cleanses. Over and over. At first, I ignored them. But the nudge wouldn't go away, something in me *knew* I needed to pay attention.

So, I did what I always do when I feel that intuitive pull: I followed it gently. I didn't jump in recklessly. I listened. I researched. I decided to do the cleanse naturally, using herbs I was familiar with, oregano oil and a wormwood tincture I made myself.

Within just a few days, though, I started feeling terrible. I knew about die-off symptoms, but this felt different. Heavier. Darker. Off.

So, I went to my GP. I explained that I started a natural herbal parasite cleanse and that something didn't feel right. I asked for

Ivermectin as I knew from research that is was the safest drug to use and it is systemic and would kill off the parasites, wherever they were in my body.

Because of the controversy surrounding Ivermectin during the COVID period, my GP wouldn't prescribe it. Instead, she prescribed Albendazole.

I took one dose, and within hours, I started feeling depressed. Over the next couple of days, it got worse. Suicidal thoughts began creeping in. And I knew something was very, very wrong. This wasn't emotional. It wasn't mental. I was not in a depressed state before. This came from *somewhere else*.

And that's when my intuition spoke loudly and clearly:
**Toxoplasma gondii.**
Toxo. The cat parasite.

I didn't even know I knew that. But I trusted the download, and when I researched the symptoms, it all lined up.

This parasite can create havoc in its host. *Toxoplasma gondii* doesn't just live in the body; it can take over the host's brain, altering behaviour in ways that serve its own life cycle. One well-known example is how it affects mice. When infected, the mouse loses its natural fear of cats and actually becomes *attracted* to cat urine. It begins to seek out the very animal that will kill and eat it, all so the parasite can complete its reproductive cycle inside the cat's gut. It's not cute. It's not quirky. It's mind control. So, all those cute videos of mice running after cats are not so cute; they are infected.

Now imagine what something like that could do in a human nervous system, in my brain, especially if left undetected. That was the moment I knew something other than my own thoughts was taking over, and I trusted my intuition to guide me out.

I went to another GP and explained what I believed was happening. She also refused to prescribe what I knew I needed. I felt blocked at every turn, but I wasn't giving up. Now, I wasn't just curious; I was certain.

**Guided to the Cure**

In the depths of that dark moment, still trusting my intuition, I "stumbled across" a video of a man talking about a paste he'd used that helped with the exact same symptoms I was experiencing. I can't publicly share what the product was, but I'll just say, I did my research. I sourced the paste. I took a single dose. Within an hour, the suicidal thoughts lifted. Within a day, the depression was gone. And within two days, I felt better than I had in *years*.

This journey didn't make sense to anyone else. I didn't have lab results. I didn't have external validation. I had something more powerful, a *yes* in my body that kept leading me toward healing.

That's the power of intuition.

It's subtle, but strong. It's often the first whisper before your logical mind steps in to override it. And when you learn to hear it and *honour* it, your entire approach to healing changes.

Sometimes your soul knows before your body does. Sometimes your gut knows what your doctor doesn't. Intuition doesn't replace action; it *guides* it.

**Practices for Awareness-Based Healing**

Awareness and intuition are not abstract ideas; they are practical, powerful tools that you can use every single day to reconnect with your body and activate healing from the inside out.

This isn't about becoming obsessive or "doing it right." It's about learning to relate to your body with curiosity, presence, and compassion. These practices are simple, but they are potent. When used regularly, they begin to rewire your relationship with your symptoms and with yourself.

**Daily Body Awareness Check-In**

This simple practice brings you back into a relationship with your body.

**Try this once a day, even for just 3 minutes:**

1. Close your eyes. Take a deep breath and let it out slowly.

2. Ask: *What's happening in my body right now?*

3. Scan from head to toe and notice any areas of:

- Tightness

- Discomfort

- Numbness

- Heat or cold

- Movement or stillness

4. Ask: *What might this part of my body be trying to say?*

5. Place your hand over that area and simply acknowledge it

   *I'm here. I'm listening.*

You don't need to fix anything, just listen.


**Awareness Through Language**
Start paying attention to the words you use when talking about your health or body. Each time you catch yourself saying, *"I have..."* or *"I'm always..."*, pause.

Ask:

- Is this a temporary experience or am I turning it into an

identity?

- What would change if I said, *"I'm recovering from..."* or *"My body is healing..."*?

This alone can shift the way your subconscious mind engages with healing.

**Track Your Body's Signals**

Keep a journal (or a note on your phone) where you jot down:

- Any recurring physical symptoms
- What you ate and how it made you feel.
- What were you thinking or experiencing emotionally when you felt the discomfort in your body.

Over time, you'll start seeing patterns that connect your physical state to your emotional and energetic state. These patterns are gold. They help you *respond* instead of react.

**Translation Prompt**

Each time you feel something in your body, ask:

- *If this symptom could talk, what would it say?*
- *What emotion or memory might be stored here?*
- *Is there a phrase I use that reflects what I'm feeling?*

(Go back to the list of body phrases from earlier if you need help.)

**Closing Reflection Questions**

- What is one area of my body I've been ignoring or avoiding?
- What might that part of me need: attention, rest, expression, love?
- If I trusted that my body was on my side, how would I treat it differently?

Awareness doesn't always provide instant answers. But it does give you a starting point. It shifts you out of helplessness and into a relationship. Intuition becomes the compass that keeps guiding you forward, not into fear, but into wholeness.

Your body is not broken. It's brilliant.

You don't need to master every tool or practice. Just begin with presence. One breath. One check-in. One moment of choosing to listen instead of overriding.

Healing begins there.

**From Inner Healing to Interpersonal Harmony**
Healing your relationship with your body is one of the most intimate and profound journeys you'll ever take. It teaches you

how to listen, how to honour, and how to trust again, not just physically, but energetically and emotionally.

As your awareness grows and your intuition sharpens, you begin to see that the same principles apply beyond the body. The way you relate to *yourself* is the foundation for how you relate to *others*.

Now that we've explored the connection between awareness, intuition, and healing, we turn our attention to the next layer of transformation, our relationships. Because once you reconnect with your inner world, you begin to see your outer world with entirely new eyes.

**Emotional Imprints (Trauma)**

We can't close this chapter without speaking to something that sits quietly beneath many of the patterns we've explored. Most of the world calls it trauma, but I call it emotional imprints or emotional scars.

When people hear the word trauma, they often think of big, life-altering events, abuse, neglect, loss, and danger. And while those experiences are indeed traumatic, they're not the only ones that leave a mark. In fact, many of the deepest imprints we carry were formed in subtle, quiet moments. Moments we didn't even realise had the power to shape us.

If you think about a scar on your body, you know there was once a wound there, some kind of injury. The size of the scar often reflects the depth of the cut. Some scars fade over time, and others remain visible or even distort the skin around them. It's the same with our emotional lives. Emotional scars are created when we go through an experience that feels overwhelming, confusing, or distressing, and we don't have the tools or support to process it in the moment. So our system does what it knows best: it adapts. It stores the tension in the body. It assigns meaning to the moment. And it files it away in the nervous system for safekeeping.

These imprints remain, not to punish us, but to protect us. But over time, what was once protection can become restriction.

Take something as seemingly small as a parent saying no. Let's say your mum usually says yes when you ask for a chocolate at the shop. But one day, she's tired, overwhelmed, distracted, and she says no. That moment lands differently. It's not just "no," it feels like "I'm not worth it today." And suddenly, a pattern forms: my needs are too much. I'm not loved. I shouldn't ask. It sounds simple. But it runs deep. That small rejection can quietly become a lifelong need for approval or a belief that you're not good enough, just like how a single comment from my maths teacher, who threw me in a bin, made me doubt my intelligence and struggle with maths for most of my life.

And just like that, the body and nervous system start adapting to the belief that you're not safe to be seen, or heard, or express your needs. That's trauma. Or rather, that's an emotional imprint.

**My Voice Was Silenced**

When I was in high school, I used to sing in the church. Sometimes as part of the band and other times as a solo. It brought me joy. It felt natural. I remember one practice session where I was listening to another young woman sing; she had this beautiful vibrato, and I was just starting to find mine. In that moment, I was inspired. I was growing. I let my voice go and added a bit of vibrato to my singing. The excitement I was feeling and the creativity I wanted to explore in that moment was cut short by my mum's voice, "Don't sing like that."

She didn't mean harm. She'd had no formal training. But those words landed like a blade. And in that instant, my voice was shut down. It played out not just in my literal voice, but my emotional voice, too.

It became an emotional scar that stayed with me for years. For the longest time, I couldn't sing. Not publicly. Not even in private. It wasn't until I'd been married nearly ten years that my then husband heard me sing for the first time.

That's the thing about imprints: they can make us bury parts of ourselves that once felt free.

Today, I use my voice in my sound healing and frequency alignment sessions. I channel it in my work, in my purpose. My voice has returned. But for the longest time, it was silenced by that one moment. That's the kind of trauma we often overlook, but it's just as powerful as the big, obvious wounds.

**Let's Talk About Therapy and Healing**

I believe therapy can be incredibly helpful. But I also believe it's become almost inaccessible to the average person. And the system itself is outdated. Well-meaning people go to study therapy and psychology because they want to help others heal. But they end up being trained in a model that limits their tools and discredits anything outside its walls.

Many therapists are told what they can and cannot say. There are strict steps they must follow, and if they step outside those lines, they risk being sued or losing their licenses. Then there are people outside that system, people who genuinely help others heal, but the moment they use terms like "social anxiety" or "post-traumatic stress," they find themselves facing legal threats. These words have been claimed and copyrighted by an industry that should be supporting healing, not gatekeeping it.

Imagine if every therapist were taught to begin by helping their clients build awareness. Just that one shift alone would cut their treatment time in half. But that wouldn't serve the systems profiting from prolonged struggle. The truth is that most people don't need medication or a "formal" diagnosis. What they need is to return to themselves. To notice what makes them feel alive and what doesn't. To begin choosing what feels right for *them*.

**Distress Without Resolve**

I'm trying to change the way people think about trauma. Because most of the time, when our adult lives aren't working, it can be traced back to an emotional imprint we experienced as children. Most imprints occur before the age of 8, 9, or 10. During those formative years, we experience the world not through logic but sensation and felt meaning. So when something distressing happens and we don't have the tools or support to resolve it, our system adapts. We survive it. But those adaptations don't always serve us long-term.

That's the definition I want people to remember: trauma is distress without resolve. Whether it was a violent event or something as subtle as emotional neglect, what matters is that we were left to make sense of it alone. We internalised it. And now we're living out the adaptations we made to survive it.

**The Identity Crisis That Follows**

This is why healing can sometimes feel disorienting. When you begin to resolve your imprints, your survival self begins to fall away, and your authentic self starts to rise. But if you've lived your whole life as a people pleaser, or as the quiet one, or the overachiever, then suddenly not reacting in those ways anymore can feel like an identity crisis. You start questioning your desires, your reactions, even your wardrobe. You look around and wonder if the life you've built is actually yours. It's confronting. But it's also liberating.

Most of us have built our lives around the version of us that knew how to stay safe. But that's not the version of us that knows how to be free.

**It's Time to Heal Differently**

It's time we started approaching mental health and healing from a spiritual perspective, not just a psychological one. Emotional scars aren't meant to be hidden away in shame. They're meant to be acknowledged. They soften when tended to. And just like the skin around a scar can eventually smooth again, your nervous system and your sense of self can return to peace.

Your imprints are not here to define you. They're here to guide you back home.

**From Imprint to Intimacy - Healing Before Connection**

Healing your emotional imprints is one of the most sacred and life-altering journeys you'll ever take. It's not just about feeling better, it's about remembering who you were before the adaptations, before the shutdowns, before the world taught you to be smaller than you truly are.

It teaches you how to honour your past without being owned by it. How to trust the quiet voice within. How to meet the parts of yourself you once buried with softness instead of shame.

And as your awareness deepens and your intuition strengthens, something profound begins to happen: the way you relate to others changes too.

Because every relationship you have is a mirror of the one you have with yourself.

Now that we've explored emotional imprints, protective patterns, and the journey back to wholeness, we're ready to explore the next layer of transformation: our relationships. Once you begin healing from within, you'll start to experience connection in a whole new way.

**In This Chapter, We Explored…**

• How healing is not linear but layered, a journey of uncovering rather than fixing.
• The way early subconscious beliefs and trauma can shape our relationship with the body.
• How symptoms are often messengers, not problems, pointing us toward deeper truths.
• The importance of the language we use when talking about our health and why *not claiming* a diagnosis matters.
• How intuition can lead us to solutions our mind can't yet explain, and how it guided me through a powerful healing experience.
• The hidden wisdom in common body-related expressions and how to use them to better understand your own body.
• Practical awareness practices to help you listen to, care for, and reconnect with your body in a deeper way.
• Emotional imprints and how they are simply there to guide us, not harm us.

Healing begins when we choose to listen. And the more we do, the more the body, mind, and soul begin to move in harmony.

## CHAPTER 8

## AWARENESS IN RELATIONSHIPS AND PARTNERSHIPS

> *"Until you make the unconscious conscious, it will direct your life, and you will call it fate."*
> *-Carl Jung*

We need to bring it back to basics.

Relationships have become complicated, not because love is hard, but because we've drifted away from the fundamentals that make love last. We've forgotten how to be present. How to be honest. How to be truly aware of ourselves and each other.

Most people don't struggle in relationships because they've stopped loving each other. They struggle because they've stopped *seeing* each other. They've stopped showing up with curiosity. They've stopped listening for what's unspoken. They've stopped pausing to ask, *"What's really going on here?"*

We get caught up in the day-to-day, routines, responsibilities, roles, and before we know it, the relationship becomes something we manage, not something we nurture. It becomes a list of tasks or expectations, instead of a sacred space to connect and grow.

That's where awareness comes in.

Awareness is how we begin to truly see each other again.

It's how we return to ourselves *and* to each other. It's what allows us to notice the little things, the energy behind a comment, the shift in someone's tone, the walls being built before words are even spoken. Awareness is what slows things down so we can hear, feel, and connect with what's real.

When you bring awareness into a relationship, everything changes.

There's more space. More breath. More choice.

You begin to respond rather than react. You pause instead of pounce. You listen instead of defend. You observe your own patterns without shame, and you start to see your partner through a clearer lens, too.

Awareness lets you meet your relationship in real-time, not through the filters of your past pain or future fears. It gives you the ability to hold your emotions without dumping them. It allows for intimacy without enmeshment, honesty without cruelty, and clarity without control.

**Unconscious Relationship Patterns**

Most people walk into relationships carrying silent agreements and invisible expectations they're not even aware of. These patterns often stem from childhood conditioning, past heartbreaks, unhealed wounds, or cultural programming. And unless we bring them into the light, they will quietly run the show.

Here are five of the most common unconscious patterns that show up in relationships, and how awareness helps shift them.

**1. "If they loved me, they'd just know."**
This belief is rooted in the fantasy that love should be intuitive and effortless, that our partner should somehow be able to *read our minds*. When they don't, we feel hurt, unloved, or overlooked, when in reality, we just haven't communicated clearly.

**The trap:** Expecting your partner to anticipate your needs without ever voicing them.

**The shift with awareness:** You begin to see that expecting mind-reading is unfair to both of you. Awareness invites you to take responsibility for expressing what you need with clarity and compassion. You stop resenting and start relating.

**2. "It's your job to make me happy."**
This creates enormous pressure in a relationship. When we expect our partner to be the source of our happiness, we hand

over our emotional power. And when they inevitably fall short, we blame them for our inner emptiness.

**The trap:** Outsourcing your emotional well-being to someone else.

**The shift with awareness:** You begin to recognise that happiness is an inside job. Instead of demanding joy from your partner, you start nurturing it within yourself, and your relationship becomes a space of sharing, not saving.

### 3. "If we argue, something's wrong with us."

Many people equate conflict with failure. But healthy conflict can be a doorway to deeper connection, *if* you know how to navigate it consciously. Avoiding conflict at all costs often leads to emotional suppression and resentment.

**The trap:** Believing that love should always feel easy and peaceful.

**The shift with awareness:** You begin to see arguments as growth points, not deal-breakers. You learn to stay present through discomfort, to listen with curiosity, and to use conflict as a mirror rather than a weapon.

**Note:** Of course, there are exceptions. If you are being abused, you should seek help.

### 4. "You're responsible for my triggers."

When something our partner does brings up pain or discomfort, it's easy to assume they're to blame. But triggers are usually a sign of something unhealed within us. Without awareness, we project our pain onto our partner instead of owning it.

**The trap:** Making your partner responsible for your emotions.
**The shift with awareness:** You begin to notice your triggers instead of reacting from them. You can pause, reflect, and ask, *"Where is this really coming from?"* Instead of accusing, you share from your truth, and open the door to healing.

### 5. "I have to earn love by performing."

This pattern often stems from childhood experiences where love was conditional, based on behaviour, achievement, or people-pleasing. As adults, we carry this into relationships, believing we must prove our worth to be loved.

**The trap:** Over-giving, people pleasing, over-functioning, or losing yourself in the relationship.
**The shift with awareness:** You begin to see that love doesn't require sacrifice or self-abandonment. You learn to receive love *as you are*, not as you perform. From this space, you begin to build relationships that feel safe, mutual, and real.

Awareness helps you spot these inherited patterns and gently bring them to the surface. You begin to see where your automatic reactions come from, and instead of letting those reactions drive your behaviour, you create space to choose something new.

Instead of expecting your partner to meet your every emotional need, you begin meeting yourself first. Then, from that fullness, you can love more freely, with fewer conditions and more presence.

Here's an exercise that will help you start the process of becoming aware in your relationship.

**Exercise: Spot the Pattern**

Before we can change a pattern, we have to name it.

Take a moment to reflect on your own relationship history, whether you're currently in a partnership or reflecting on past ones. Bring awareness to where you might still be operating from an unconscious place.

**Ask yourself:**

1. What are some things I expect from my partner that I haven't clearly communicated?

2. Do I ever feel resentful for not getting something that I never actually asked for?

3. When I feel triggered in a relationship, what's my first instinct: to blame, withdraw, control, or prove?

4. Have I been trying to earn love by being perfect, giving too much, or abandoning my own needs?

5.     Where have I handed over responsibility for my happiness?

Write down any patterns you notice. Then gently ask yourself:

"What would this look like if I showed up with awareness instead?"

This simple shift in attention, from reaction to reflection, is the beginning of transformation. It's not about judging yourself. It's about seeing clearly... so you can choose consciously.

**Relationships Aren't Meant to Hurt You**

We've been taught that love should be dramatic. That it should take us to the edge, break us open, and somehow put us back together again. But that's not love. That's unresolved pain being played out through intimacy.

True love doesn't hurt; it heals.

That doesn't mean relationships are always easy or comfortable. But pain isn't the point. Growth is. And when you meet a relationship with awareness, you begin to see that every conflict, every frustration, and every emotional wave isn't here to destroy the connection, it's here to refine it.

Relationships will trigger you. That's not always a sign that something's wrong. It's a beautiful gift to show you where you can clear more hurt from your past to make space for the love in your future.

When you're unaware, it's easy to get stuck in the mess of it all, the assumptions, the defensiveness, the stories from your past playing out in real time. You spiral into the same arguments. You speak from your wounds instead of your wisdom.

But when you're aware, you see the pattern *as* it's happening. You catch yourself in the middle of the reaction and choose a different response. You pause, breathe, and remember:

*This isn't about winning. This is about understanding.*

Each challenge becomes an invitation to grow together instead of tearing each other down. The goal is not perfection, but partnership. Not being right but being real. Not proving but practicing presence.

Awareness turns the battlefield into sacred ground. And the most beautiful part? You don't need both people to be perfectly self-aware for this to work. Your presence alone can shift the dynamic. When you show up differently, the relationship can't stay the same.

### The Sacred Pause

Every relationship reaches moments where something is said, a line is crossed, or an old wound is touched, and suddenly, you're flooded with emotion. It's in these moments that most relationships either spiral or shift.

The Sacred Pause is the practice that creates the difference.

When you feel yourself getting triggered, when your chest tightens, your voice rises, your thoughts race, or you shut down, that is your cue. That's the moment to stop, breathe, and *pause*.

The Sacred Pause is not about avoidance. It's not silent treatment. It's not checking out.

It's a conscious choice to step back and *tune in*.

Instead of reacting from pain, habit, or survival mode, you pause to say something like:

"Something's coming up inside me, and I just need a moment. I'm becoming aware of something in me that wants to react, and I want to understand what it is before I respond."

That single moment of awareness can prevent hours of misunderstanding.

**What Happens During the Pause**

When you pause, you're not suppressing. You're creating space to *observe*. You give yourself the opportunity to check in:

- **What am I actually feeling right now?** (Not just anger, but maybe hurt. Not just defensiveness, but fear.)

- **What is this reminding me of?** (Is this about my partner, or is this familiar from childhood?)
- **What do I need right now?** (Reassurance? Space? Clarity?)

This moment of reflection helps you return to the conversation grounded, rather than reactive.

**Why It Works**

Your nervous system doesn't differentiate between emotional threat and physical threat. When you're triggered in a relationship, your body often shifts into fight, flight, freeze, or fawn. That's not bad, it's protective. But it's not always helpful in love.

The Sacred Pause interrupts that automatic response. It helps you move from a reactive state to a responsive one. It bridges the gap between your unconscious reaction and your conscious choice.

**Real-Life Examples**

**Example 1: The Misunderstood Comment**
Your partner makes a joke, and you instantly feel embarrassed or hurt. Instead of snapping back or withdrawing, you say,

"That landed in a way I didn't expect. I want to check in with myself before we keep talking."

You take a moment. You realise the reaction was about past experiences of being ridiculed in public. With that awareness, you're able to come back and say,

"I know you didn't mean anything by that, but it touched an old nerve. Can we talk about it?"

**Example 2: The Silent Resentment**
You're cooking dinner again, even though you agreed to share the load. Instead of slamming pots and fuming in silence, you pause. You ask yourself, *Why am I angry?* You realise you've been carrying more than you voiced.

Instead of exploding later, you bring it up calmly and clearly.

That's the power of the pause. It lets you check in with the *real* issue, so you don't cause more damage reacting to the surface one.

**Bringing Your Partner In**

What makes this tool even more powerful is when you use it *with* your partner instead of walking away in silence. You're not abandoning the moment, you're co-creating a safe space.

By saying, "I'm noticing something's coming up in me, and I want to make sense of it before we keep going," you model emotional responsibility. You invite your partner into your self-awareness. You show them it's not *them*, it's something within *you* that's asking to be seen.

Over time, this builds trust. It softens defences. And it shows your partner that emotional intensity doesn't have to mean disconnection.

**Communicate, Don't Project**

Learning the difference between expressing and projecting is one of the most powerful shifts you can make in any relationship.

Most people think they're communicating when really, they're just offloading.
They're venting without clarity.
They're reacting instead of reflecting.
They're speaking from their wounds instead of their truth.

When that happens, conversations turn into emotional landmines. One person explodes, the other shuts down. Walls go up, hearts close, and nothing gets resolved. Over time, resentment grows, not necessarily from the problems themselves, but from the way those problems are handled.

That's why *awareness* is the foundation for real, honest, healing communication.

**What Does It Look Like to Project?**

- You blame your partner for your emotions: *"You made me feel this way."*
- You speak in absolutes: *"You never listen." "You always do this."*
- You unload your frustration without context or reflection:

    *"I can't take this anymore!"* (without explaining what "this" is)
- You expect them to fix something you haven't even articulated.

Projection is what happens when we speak *from* our pain rather than *about* it.

**What Does Conscious Communication Sound Like?**

Instead of projecting, you pause. You check in. You own your experience.

You say things like:

- "I noticed I felt really hurt when that happened, and I'm trying to make sense of why."

- "What you said reminded me of something from my past, and I think that's why I reacted the way I did."
- "Right now, I feel overwhelmed, and I don't want to take it out on you. Can we talk about it when I've had a moment to breathe?"

Conscious communication doesn't mean sugar-coating the truth. It means speaking it in a way that invites connection instead of disconnection.

**Speak to Be Understood, Not Just to Be Heard**

Most people speak to *defend*, not to connect. They're trying to be right instead of real.

But real communication is less about proving a point and more about *revealing a truth*. It's about making your inner world visible to someone else in a way they can actually receive.

That's why one of the most powerful questions you can ask in a tense moment is:

*"What did you hear when I said that?"*

Because more often than not, they didn't hear what you *meant*. They heard it through their own filters, their past, their fears, their wounds. This question opens the door to clarity. It gives both of you a chance to correct misunderstandings *before* they turn into unnecessary arguments.

## Feel First, Then Speak

One of the best pieces of advice I can give is this: Feel your feelings before you speak them. Take a moment. Breathe. Let the emotion run through you without judging it or acting on it. Then speak from the clarity beneath the charge. You'll find that your words carry more truth, and your partner will be more likely to listen and your relationship will start to feel safer, more honest, and far less reactive.

## Am I Projecting or Communicating?

### A Quick Awareness Checklist

Next time you're in a heated moment, pause and check in with yourself using the list below.

**You're likely projecting if:**

- You're speaking from emotional charge without reflection.
- You feel the need to *blame* or *prove* something.
- You're using words like *"always"*, *"never"*, or *"you make me..."*.
- You're focused more on being *right* than being *understood*.
- You haven't asked yourself *why* you're feeling the way you do.

**You're likely communicating if:**

- You've paused and checked in with your own emotional state first.
- You're using "I" language: *"I feel... I'm noticing... I need..."*
- You're expressing curiosity, not control.
- You're open to hearing your partner's perspective, not just delivering yours.
- You're speaking from clarity, not chaos.

**Remember:**
You don't need to be perfect.
You just need to be *present*.
Every time you catch yourself projecting and choose instead to communicate consciously, you're changing the relationship, for the better.

**Love Is Giving, Not Taking**

Somewhere along the way, we got relationships all wrong.

We began to believe that the purpose of love is to fill something in us. To complete us. To meet all our needs. To take away our loneliness, our insecurity, our fear of being unseen.

Without realising it, many of us approach relationships from a subtle undercurrent of *"What can I get?"*

- Can you make <u>me</u> feel safe?
- Can you make <u>me</u> feel wanted?
- Can you show up for <u>me</u> in the ways I haven't yet learned to show up for myself?

But real love doesn't come from taking. Real love comes from giving, freely, consciously, without scorekeeping. This doesn't mean becoming a martyr or abandoning your own needs. It means shifting the *intention* behind how you show up.

**Love Is in the Small Things**

Love is less about the grand gestures and more about the small, thoughtful moments where presence meets intention.

If your partner loves the ocean, and you make the effort to walk on the beach with them, even if saltwater and sand isn't your thing, that's love.

If you love movies and they sit through a film with you, not because they care about the plot but because *you* care, that's love.

These are not transactions.
They're invitations.
To step outside of your preferences and into shared presence.
To *see* the other person, not through the lens of what they can

give you, but through the lens of who they are and what lights them up.

That's love in motion.

## From Self-Centred to Soul-Centred

Most relationships suffer not from a lack of love, but from a lack of self-awareness in how that love is expressed.

When you're unconscious, you love from a self-centred space, which sounds like:

- "Why aren't you doing this for me?"
- "I gave to you, now where's mine?"
- "You're not making me happy."

But when you're awake, you begin to love from a soul-centred space, and that sounds like:

- "How can I serve this connection with truth?"
- "How can I honour myself *and* love you well?"
- "What would love choose right now?"

It's not about keeping a tally.
It's about *becoming* the kind of person who gives from love, not obligation.

And here's the beautiful paradox:
The more you give from that selfless space, the more you tend to receive, not from a place of demand, but from a natural overflow.

**Selfless Doesn't Mean Self-Abandoning**

Let's be clear: giving in love doesn't mean losing yourself. It doesn't mean becoming a doormat, people-pleasing, or tolerating poor behaviour in the name of "being loving."

True giving comes *after* self-connection, not in place of it.

When you are deeply rooted in your own awareness and intuition, your giving becomes wise, nourishing, and sustainable. It comes from overflow, not depletion.

**How Do I Give and Receive Love?**

Every person has their own unique way of giving and receiving love. But without awareness, we often default to giving love the way *we* like to receive it, rather than tuning into what actually nourishes the other person.

You might express love through words, but your partner feels loved through acts of service.
You might crave physical closeness, while they feel most connected through shared time or deep conversation.
This mismatch doesn't mean you're incompatible; it just means you need more awareness.

This is why presence matters. This is why awareness matters. It helps you attune to your partner's needs, not just your own needs.

Giving love consciously means:

- Paying attention to how <u>they</u> feel safest and most seen.
- Noticing what lights <u>them</u> up, and not needing it to match how you would do it.
- Asking: *What helps them feel loved? And how can I meet that need in a way that also honours me?*

Receiving love consciously means:

- Allowing yourself to be loved in the ways they *can* express it, even if it's different from your ideal.
- Communicating what you need clearly, without shame.
- Being open to love, showing up in forms you might not have expected.

**Quick Reflection:**

Ask yourself and journal on the following:

- How do I naturally tend to show love in a relationship?
- Where did I learn that this was the "right" way to love?
- How do I feel most loved and seen?
- Have I ever expected my partner to love me the way I love them?

- What might shift if I truly *observed* how they give and receive love?

Awareness is the bridge between what's unconscious and what's possible.

When you become aware of your patterns and theirs, you can begin to love more consciously and be loved more deeply.

## When Awareness Says It's Time to Walk Away

Sometimes, the most loving thing you can do for yourself and the other person is to leave.

We don't talk about this enough. Commitment is beautiful, but staying when something is no longer aligned can quietly erode your spirit. Not every relationship is meant to last. Some are bridges. Some are teachers. Some are chapters. And sometimes, even when the love was real, it's time to let go.

I know this because I lived it.

## My Own Spiral

I got married in 2005 in South Africa. We moved to Australia a year later while I was six months pregnant. We were still in love and excited for the new chapter. But the move, the isolation from family, and the intensity of new parenthood took a toll on us. And beneath it all, something deeper was unfolding.

I was growing spiritually, emotionally, and energetically. My then-husband, however, stayed exactly the same. Not in a bad way. Just... unchanged. Unmoved. Unwilling to look within, while I was on a constant path of awakening.

For the last five years of our marriage, leading up to 2017, patterns kept repeating themselves. The same fights. The same emotional disconnection. The same feeling of being more like a housemate and caretaker than a partner. I started emotionally detaching long before we officially separated. I was going through the motions of motherhood and marriage, but inside I was slowly leaving.

In June 2016, I called it. I couldn't do it anymore.

We stood in the kitchen and had the conversation. We both admitted we weren't happy. We agreed to divorce. There was no screaming or dramatics, just a quiet truth rising to the surface.

But the next morning, he came back to me in tears. He promised to try harder. He wanted to make it work, and because part of me still loved the idea of what we had once been, I said yes.

One year later, nothing had changed.

I found myself in the exact same place again. The spiral. The loop. The inner knowing that kept whispering, *"It's time."* My intuition was shouting. My body was tired. My awareness was undeniable. But I still held on. Because that's what we do when we confuse hope with truth. When we fear regret more than we trust our own inner voice. When we want to give someone "one more chance," even though we already know we've given them many.

Eventually, I listened, and the moment I did, I remembered who I was. Not just a partner, or a mother, or a caretaker, but a woman with a soul that could no longer stay asleep inside a life that didn't fit.

**Intuition Already Knows**
Most people in misaligned or unhealthy relationships already know, deep down, that something isn't quite right. There's a quiet sense of unease that lingers beneath the surface, sometimes subtle, sometimes loud, but always present.

They feel it in their gut, even if they can't explain why. They hear it in the silence between conversations, in the heaviness that follows certain interactions. They see it in their partner's eyes, an absence, a disconnection, a tension that never fully leaves. They notice it in the way the same unresolved issues keep circling back, never truly moving forward.

Intuition can be inconvenient. It often points to truths we're not ready to face. And so, we override it. We talk ourselves out of it. We rationalise what we feel. We excuse what we see. We delay the inevitable. We deny what we know.

If you're in that space right now, let me say this clearly:

If your awareness and intuition are whispering that something isn't right, **listen**.
If your body feels heavy, tense, or constantly depleted, **listen**.
If your soul feels smaller in their presence than it does on your own, **listen**.

That quiet knowing inside of you is not trying to ruin your life. It's trying to *restore* it.
It's not there to shame you.
It's there to show you the way back to yourself.

**When It's Abusive**

If you are in a relationship that is emotionally, mentally, or physically abusive, please hear this clearly: this is not your lesson to stay and learn from. You are not meant to suffer in the name of growth. This is not your karma to carry, and it is not your job to endure pain in order to prove your strength or loyalty.

In these situations, your awareness and intuition are often already trying to speak to you, sometimes gently, sometimes with urgency. You might feel it in your body every time they walk into the room. You might hear it as a quiet but persistent voice inside, saying, "This *isn't right.*" But fear, shame, or uncertainty can keep you silent. It can keep you stuck.

You might not know how to leave. You might not feel strong enough yet. The path out may feel confusing or terrifying, especially if you've been isolated, manipulated, or made to question your own reality.

But you don't need to have it all figured out to begin.

Start with awareness. Acknowledge what you're feeling. Start with intuition. Trust what your body and inner knowing have been telling you.

And then, just take one step.

That step might be speaking your truth out loud for the first time.
It might be setting a boundary, calling a friend, or simply writing it down in your journal.
It might be the moment you say, *"I don't deserve this,"* and start to believe it.

The shift doesn't begin with leaving. It begins with seeing clearly.
And from there, the next step will always reveal itself.

### The Role of Intuition in Relationships

Awareness helps you *see*. Intuition helps you *know*.

Together, they form the inner compass that guides you through the complexities of love, connection, and communication. And while awareness is more observational, focused on what's happening in the present, intuition often points to the *truth beneath the surface*, sometimes before anything visible has happened at all.

Your intuition is the part of you that senses what words don't say.
It picks up on the energy in the room.
It hears the pause between the sentences.
It notices the vibe that shifts when something's not quite right, even if everything looks fine on paper.

### Intuition Isn't Loud, But It's Clear

It's not always dramatic. It doesn't scream. It often comes as a gentle inner nudge, a soft whisper, a tightness in the chest, or a quiet sense of "something's off."

Sometimes it shows up as unease before a difficult conversation, even if nothing has been said yet.
Sometimes it's a subtle contraction in your body when someone says, *"I'm fine."*

Sometimes it's a knowing that this connection isn't right for you, even though there's no "logical" reason.

If you're not tuned in, it's easy to ignore or override these signals. But over time, ignoring intuition leads to disconnection from yourself and from the truth.

**Why Intuition Gets Dismissed**

One of the most common reasons people struggle in relationships isn't because they don't have access to truth, it's because they're ignoring the truth their intuition is already offering them.

In many cases, intuition is dismissed not because it's unclear, but because it's *uncomfortable*. Deep down, you might already know something isn't aligned. You might sense that the relationship is no longer growing, that something isn't working, or that your needs are not being met in a healthy way. But acknowledging that truth often requires change. And change can be confronting.

We want to believe the best in the people we love.
We want the relationship to succeed.
We want to avoid hard conversations, conflict, and pain.
We fear making waves, hurting someone, being blamed, or having to walk away from something familiar, even if it's no longer right.

So instead of listening to our intuition, we override it.

We tell ourselves we're being too sensitive.
We convince ourselves it will get better.
We wait for more evidence, more signs, more certainty, when deep down, we already *know*.

Ignoring your inner knowing never leads to peace.
It only leads to prolonged discomfort, deeper disconnection, and often, regret.

Intuition doesn't try to convince you.
It doesn't present a list of logical reasons.
It doesn't raise its voice to get your attention.

It simply offers a quiet but firm truth, and waits for you to listen.

You don't need to understand *why* you feel what you feel right away. You just need to stop dismissing the feeling altogether. Because the more you honour your inner knowing, the louder and clearer it becomes. And the more you delay it, the heavier everything starts to feel.

**Intuition and the Dating App Moment**
I experienced one of those unmistakable, intuitive moments myself, not in some dramatic life event, but in an ordinary situation that turned into something meaningful.

I was chatting to a man on a dating app. The conversation was light, casual, and nothing overtly wrong was being said. At the same time, on a different screen, I was deep in a separate conversation with someone about awareness and intuition, two things that have become central to how I live, teach, and guide others.

And then it happened.

I had what I can only describe as an out-of-body experience. It was as if I zoomed out and saw myself from above. On one side, I was speaking about alignment, spiritual depth, awareness and intuition. On the other side, I was giving energy to a man who, if I was honest, didn't feel aligned at all.

The contrast was so clear. It was jarring.

In that moment, something inside me clicked. It wasn't dramatic or loud, but it was absolutely certain.

*He's not your guy.*

There was no need to rationalise it or wait for more evidence. I could feel the misalignment in my body, and I knew I didn't want to continue the conversation. So, I ended it. Gracefully. Clearly. Without guilt.

And just a few minutes later, his words confirmed what I had already sensed. The energy shifted, and I saw who he really was. But my intuition had already told me, long before he did. That's the power of awareness and intuition working together.

Awareness saved me time.
Intuition saved me from heartache.
And together, they brought me back into alignment with myself.

This is exactly what I mean when I say that awareness and intuition are your personal superpowers. When you let them guide you, you no longer have to learn every lesson through pain. You learn through presence. You protect your energy. And you honour what you know, before it costs you.

**What Am I practising in This Relationship?**

Every relationship is a mirror, reflecting back the parts of ourselves we're aware of, and the parts we've yet to fully meet. But more than that, every relationship is also a practice.

Whether you realise it or not, you are always rehearsing something in the way you show up.
Through your actions, your responses, your silences, and your habits, you are practicing patterns. Over time, those patterns become your way of being in the relationship.

You may be practising patience, or you may be practising control.
You might be practising honest self-expression, or unconsciously reinforcing self-abandonment.
You could be practising emotional openness or defaulting to

defensiveness.

You might be nurturing compassion or performing for approval.

You may be deepening your capacity for love, or silently reinforcing old patterns of fear.

The point of this reflection is not to judge yourself. It's to *wake up* to how you're actually participating in the relationship dynamic, because that participation is powerful.

Whatever you practice most often becomes your emotional default.

Whatever you reinforce consistently becomes your relational identity.

So, if you find yourself asking, *"Why does this keep happening?"*

A more revealing question might be, *"What have I been practising without realising it?"*

This is where awareness becomes your ally, because once you see the pattern, you are no longer trapped inside it. You can choose again. You can practice something new.

And in doing so, you don't just change the relationship, you change yourself within it.

**Bringing Awareness to Your Habits**

When we don't pause to reflect, we automatically default to

what's most familiar. And familiarity doesn't always mean healthy. It just means *practised*.

You may find yourself walking on eggshells in your relationship, not because your partner is necessarily unsafe, but because somewhere along the way, you learned that anger leads to punishment, withdrawal, or chaos. So now, without even realising it, you tiptoe. You avoid. You silence yourself to keep the peace.

Or maybe you keep giving more than you have to offer, overextending emotionally, energetically, or even physically, because you were taught that love must be earned. Maybe if you just do more, give more, prove yourself more, *then* you'll be worthy of love in return.

You might even test your partner's love without meaning to, pulling away, creating tension, or waiting for them to fail, just to see if they'll leave. Not because you want them to, but because a deeper part of you is terrified of being vulnerable enough to say, *"I need you to stay."*

These are not flaws.
These are *learned survival patterns*.
They are ways your nervous system tries to keep you safe in relationships, often long before you had the tools to choose something different.

But here's the key: they are still just that, patterns.

And patterns can be shifted. But only when they're seen clearly.

That's what awareness does. It brings your automatic habits into conscious light. It gives you the power to choose again.

You don't have to keep practising the same roles you learned as a child, or the same survival strategies you used in past relationships.
You can notice them, meet them with compassion, and decide to show up differently, on purpose.

**A Powerful Daily Question**

At any moment in your relationship, you can pause and ask:

**"What am I practising right now?"**

- Am I practising reaction or response?
- Am I practising honesty or hiding?
- Am I practising listening or waiting to defend myself?
- Am I practising control or trust?
- Am I practising fear… or am I practising love?

This one question can change the entire dynamic of a conversation, a disagreement, or a relationship pattern.

**Choose to Practice Something New**
The most liberating truth about awareness is that it gives you

back your choice. You are not trapped in your old patterns, no matter how deeply ingrained they are. You are not bound to replay the same relationship dynamics you witnessed growing up. You are not required to carry forward the beliefs, behaviours, or survival strategies you once used to keep yourself safe. You don't have to be who you were in your last relationship. You don't even have to be who you were yesterday.

Every single moment offers a doorway to something new.

You can practice pausing, even when everything in you wants to react. You can practice asking for clarity before jumping to conclusions. You can practice speaking honestly about your needs, even if your voice shakes and your heart pounds. You can practice loving with boundaries, honouring both your heart and your wholeness, instead of giving from guilt or fear. You can practice trusting your own voice, even when others don't understand or validate it. You are never stuck. Not when you're aware. Because awareness invites you to evolve, on purpose. It gives you the space to choose again, and again, and again… until a new way of being becomes your new foundation.

You don't have to get it perfect. You just have to get present.

That's the real practice. That's the real power.

## Close the Gaps or They'll Be Filled by Something Else

In every relationship, no matter how strong or connected, there are moments of distance. These aren't always dramatic. Often, they're quiet, subtle spaces that open up when something is left unsaid, when a gesture is missed, or when emotional needs go unacknowledged.

These are the *gaps*.

They can be as simple as a conversation that didn't happen, a question that wasn't asked, or a feeling that wasn't shared. And while one moment may seem small on its own, when these gaps accumulate, day after day, week after week, they begin to change the texture of the relationship.

If we don't bring awareness to those gaps and tend to them with care, presence, and honest attention, *something else* will inevitably move in to fill the space.

Sometimes it's assumptions, stories we create in our minds about what the other person is thinking or feeling, without ever checking if they're true.
Sometimes it's resentment, the quiet bitterness that builds when our needs go unmet, and we don't feel safe or clear enough to express them.
Sometimes it's loneliness, even in the presence of the person we love.
And in some cases, it's someone else entirely, because humans

are wired for connection, and when it's missing at home, the soul goes searching.

## The Gaps Don't Start Big

These breakdowns rarely happen all at once. Most of the time, they begin slowly. So subtly you hardly notice.

It might start with no longer saying goodnight.
Or forgetting to ask how each other's day went.
It might be the way you stop holding hands on the couch, or the way you glance at your phone instead of looking each other in the eye.
It could be a moment when you want to share something, but you second-guess whether they'll really care… so you keep it to yourself.

You begin to assume your partner knows what you need, and so you stop expressing it. You stop checking in. You start existing side-by-side instead of relating heart-to-heart.

And little by little, the connection begins to fray, not because of a single catastrophe, but because of quiet, repeated neglect.

Not neglect with bad intent. Just unawareness.
Distraction.
Habit.
Emotional autopilot.

These are the moments where awareness becomes vital.
Because when you're present, you can feel the distance before it becomes a disconnection.
You can sense the silence before it turns into withdrawal.
You can notice the need before it becomes a wall.

This is how relationships are protected, not by perfection, but by conscious care.

**Intimacy Is in the Little Things**

We often think of intimacy as something big, something reserved for romantic getaways, long conversations under the stars, or passionate physical connection. But the deepest, most lasting intimacy is rarely built in those sweeping moments. It's built in the quiet, ordinary, often unnoticed gestures of everyday life.

Real intimacy lives in the small things.

It's the thoughtful message sent in the middle of a busy day, not because it's expected, but because you were thinking of them and wanted them to know.

It's the warm cup of tea made without being asked, because you remember how they like it, and you noticed they seemed a little worn out today.

It's the hand placed gently on their back as you pass by, that wordless reassurance: *I'm with you. I'm still here.*

It's the shared glance across the room, when no words are spoken but something unspoken is deeply understood.

These are the threads that weave intimacy into the fabric of daily life.
They're subtle, but powerful.
And when they're present, they nourish the connection without fanfare.
But when they disappear… we notice.

When these moments stop, not because of cruelty, but because of inattention, the relationship begins to feel hollow.

Not broken. Not angry. Just… faded.

Not because the love is gone.
But because it's been left *unattended*.

And unattended love, like any living thing, eventually begins to wilt.

That's why awareness matters so deeply. It's what keeps the small things alive. It reminds you that intimacy doesn't have to be grand to be meaningful.
It just has to be real.
And consistent.
And present.

**Awareness Helps You Close the Gaps**
When disconnection begins to creep into a relationship, the

answer isn't always more *effort*.
It's more *presence*.

We're conditioned to believe that fixing something means doing more, more talking, more planning, more trying. But in relationships, healing often doesn't come from doing more. It comes from doing the *right* things with intention.

It comes from slowing down enough to notice what's missing. From tuning in instead of pushing through.
From remembering that sometimes the most powerful repair happens in a single moment of truth-telling, not a grand emotional overhaul.

Start with gentle curiosity. Ask yourself:

- **Is there a gap between us that I've been avoiding?**

Have I sensed the distance but kept myself busy to avoid feeling it?

- **Have I stopped showing up in the small, meaningful ways?**

Have I let daily distractions replace the simple rituals that used to bring us closer?

- **Have I noticed something is off, but told myself it's probably nothing?**

Have I ignored my own intuition because naming it felt too

vulnerable?

- **What would it take to gently close the distance?**

Not to fix everything at once, but to meet the gap with honesty, care, and presence?

These are not confrontational questions. They are invitations, back to connection, back to love, back to what matters.

You don't need to have all the answers.
You don't need to fix everything overnight.

Sometimes, one small act of awareness, a soft check-in, a tender word, a moment of seeing and being seen, is enough to change the entire dynamic.

Because relationships are not held together by intensity.
They're held together by attention.

## Don't Wait for Disconnection to Wake You Up

One of the most painful realisations in relationships isn't that the love is gone, but that its true value was only seen after it had already fallen apart.

By the time the distance feels unbearable, by the time the silence feels heavy, by the time one or both people are no longer emotionally available… the connection that once felt alive has already faded.

Not because of betrayal. Not because of one major blowout. But because of the slow erosion that comes from not paying attention.

**Don't let that be your story.**

Don't wait until the relationship is on the edge of collapse before you start tending to it.
Don't wait until they're no longer reaching for your hand to remember how good it felt to hold theirs.
Don't wait until you're grieving what was to realise how much there still *could* have been, if only it had been nurtured.

Start now.
While the love is still here.
While the connection still has breath.

Pay attention to the way you greet each other in the morning. Not with autopilot words, but with presence.
Check in during the day, not just as a routine, but with real heart behind it.
Notice what lights them up and make an effort to meet them in that place, not because it's your thing, but because *they* matter.
And if you feel distance growing, don't pretend. Don't plaster over it. Speak to it.

**Awareness in love is preventative.**
It keeps the heart open.

It keeps the energy flowing.
It keeps the connection *alive*, before it becomes something you have to revive.

If you want a strong, lasting relationship, don't just show up for the big fires.
Anyone can react when things fall apart.

But true intimacy is built by those who tend to the *small sparks*, daily, quietly, consistently.

So, close the gaps.
Not out of panic, but out of love.
Before something else moves into the space you were always meant to protect.


## Relationships as a Path of Awakening

At their core, relationships are not just about love.
They're about *awakening*.

They are sacred spaces where our patterns surface, where our insecurities get stirred, and where our most deeply embedded fears, hopes, and stories are invited into the light.

Relationships have a way of pulling us into deeper honesty with ourselves because when we are close to another person, we can no longer hide in the same ways.
Our reactions, our defences, our longings, our triggers, they all rise to the surface.

This is why relationships can feel so intense.
Not because they are inherently dramatic or complex, but because they are spiritual work.

We think we're arguing about dishes left in the sink.
Or the way they used that tone.
Or who's doing more around the house?
But more often than not, we're unconsciously wrestling with something far deeper.

We're asking questions we don't always have words for:

- *Do I matter to you?*
- *Can I trust that you'll stay?*
- *Am I safe to be fully myself here?*
- *Will I still be loved if I stop performing, proving, or pleasing?*

These questions aren't surface level.
They come from the deepest parts of us, formed in childhood, shaped by past relationships, and buried under years of coping, surviving, and adapting.

And relationships bring all of this to the surface, not to punish us, but to *purify* us.
Not to break us, but to reveal us.

To show us where we still don't feel worthy.
To show us where we've abandoned ourselves for approval.

To show us what parts of us are still waiting to be healed, held, and honoured.

A conscious relationship doesn't avoid this process; it *welcomes* it.
It says, *"Let's grow together. Let's meet our edges. Let's walk into the fire, not to burn each other, but to burn away what's false."*

This is why I say relationships are a path of awakening.

They ask us to be present.
They ask us to be humble.
They ask us to look at ourselves, not just our partners, and say, *"Where am I not showing up fully? What am I projecting? What am I protecting?"*

And when both people are willing to do this work, something extraordinary happens:
The relationship becomes not just a place of love, but a container for transformation. Not just connection, but evolution.

### The Invitation of Conscious Love

When you begin to approach your relationship through the lens of awareness and intuition, everything starts to shift.

Suddenly, it's no longer about fixing or forcing. It's not about moulding the other person to fit your needs or trying to keep everything perfectly in balance. It becomes about presence. Truth. Growth.

You stop needing your partner to fill your emotional gaps, because you've begun meeting yourself in those places first. You stop reacting out of fear, old wounds, or unmet expectations, and instead, you begin responding from a grounded place of clarity and care.
You stop trying to control, change, or rescue, and start listening, seeing, and witnessing what's truly there without rearranging it.

Every disagreement becomes an opportunity to grow together instead of pulling apart. Every frustration becomes a mirror, reflecting something within you that is asking to be seen, healed, or claimed.
And every tender moment, no matter how small, becomes a sacred anchor, a reminder that love, when held with consciousness, can be both soft and strong at once.

This is the gift of conscious love.
It asks you not to perform, but to be present.
Not to be perfect, but to *participate*, honestly, openly, and fully.

**It's Not About Perfection, It's About Presence**
There is no such thing as a perfect relationship. There's no flawless formula. No single path. No universal checklist for love. And that's okay, because perfection isn't the goal.

The real goal is an honest connection.
A connection built not on polished images or constant harmony, but on the courage to show up *as you are*.
A connection grounded in self-awareness, soul-trust, and mutual care, even when it's messy, even when it's uncomfortable, even when it stretches you beyond what you thought you could hold.

So let go of the illusion that love has to look a certain way to be real.
Let go of the story that if it doesn't feel effortless, it must be wrong.
Let go of the pressure to figure it out before you open your heart.

Instead, ask yourself:

- Am I showing up with awareness?
- Am I listening to my intuition?
- Am I choosing to love, not just when it's easy, but when it's real?

That's what truly transforms a relationship.
Not waiting until everything is perfect.
Not waiting until your partner is fully on board.
Not waiting until the timing is just right.

You don't need to fix everything overnight.
You don't need to have a five-step plan.
You don't even need to know exactly where this is going.

You just need to begin with awareness.
You just need to trust your intuition.
You just need to be honest with yourself.

The rest will unfold from there.
And if you stay awake to it, it will unfold *beautifully*.

**Practice: Bringing Awareness into Your Relationship**

Awareness isn't just something you *understand*; it's something you *practice*.

The following simple steps are designed to help you show up with more presence, emotional clarity, and connection in your relationship, whether you're currently partnered or reflecting on past dynamics.

Use these prompts regularly, especially in moments of tension, disconnection, or emotional charge.

**Step 1: Pause Before You React**

"What am I feeling right now, and where do I feel it in my body?"

Start by slowing down. Catch yourself before you respond on autopilot. Take a breath. Place your hand on your chest or belly. Let yourself feel *without acting on it yet*.

**Step 2: Check In with Yourself**

"What story am I telling myself about this situation?"

Awareness invites you to notice what's really going on under the surface. Are you assuming the worst? Are you re-playing an old wound? Ask yourself if the reaction is about the present moment or something deeper.

**Step 3: Speak With Intention**

"Can I share what's true for me without blame, attack, or assumption?"

Use "I" language. Let your partner witness you instead of defending against you. You might say:

- "I'm noticing a lot is coming up for me right now."
- "That touched something in me I didn't expect. I'd love to talk about it when I've made sense of it."
- "I know that wasn't your intention, but this is what I felt…"

**Step 4: Ask for Clarity**

"What did you hear when I said that?"

This one question can save you hours of misunderstanding. You'd be surprised how often what was *meant* is not what was *received*. Let your partner reflect back on what they heard. It opens a space for clarity, correction, and connection.

**Step 5: Reflect Afterwards**

"What was I practising in that moment?"

Were you practising defensiveness or presence? Judgment or curiosity? Avoidance or courage?

Each time you reflect, you build a stronger foundation of awareness, and every time you choose differently, you begin to rewire the way you relate.

**You Don't Have to Be Perfect, Just Present**

This practice is not about saying the "right" thing or becoming a relationship expert.
It's about slowing down enough to hear yourself.
It's about learning to respond, not react.
It's about becoming the kind of person who brings peace into the relationship, not because you avoid the hard stuff, but because you meet it with awareness.

The more you do this, the more natural it becomes.

Your relationship will shift not because you changed them but because you changed the energy you bring into every moment.

**In This Chapter, We Explored…**

• How awareness creates space, softness, and clarity in relationships, allowing us to truly *see* each other again, not through filters of fear or expectation, but through presence.

• The most common unconscious patterns that show up in relationships, and how awareness helps us name, soften, and shift them, on purpose.

• The power of the Sacred Pause in moments of tension or emotional charge, and how this simple practice can transform reaction into reflection.

• The difference between projecting and communicating, and how to speak your truth in a way that invites connection rather than defensiveness.

• What it means to love from a selfless place, not by abandoning yourself, but by showing up with genuine presence and care, without keeping score.

• How intuition often knows before the mind is willing to admit it, and why listening to that quiet voice can protect your peace and honour your truth.

• How to recognise when a relationship may no longer be aligned, and the courage it takes to walk away not out of anger, but out of self-respect and soul-trust.

• Why closing the small gaps in a relationship, those everyday moments of presence, attention, and care, matters more than grand gestures.

- How every relationship is a practice, and every moment within it is an opportunity to choose awareness, to grow, and to love more consciously.
- And finally, how relationships, at their highest, are a path of awakening. They reveal our shadows, call forth our truth, and offer a sacred space for healing, evolution, and soul-deep connection.

## CHAPTER 9

## AWARENESS WITH AND IN OUR CHILDREN

> *"Give me your sons till the age of seven,
> and they'll forever be mine."*
> *- Attributed to various historical figures,
> including Jesuit educators*

It's chilling. But also, true.

By the time our children are seven, most of them have already internalised who they need to be in order to be *safe*, *loved*, and *accepted* by the world.

Sit still.
Be quiet.
Don't ask that.
Say thank you.
Don't be rude.
Don't be too much.
Don't make a fuss.

Ask permission.
Smile. Obey. Fit in.

This is the programming of a system that values compliance over curiosity, performance over presence, reputation over authenticity, and authority over inner intelligence.

Our kids are being shaped, not just by us, but by every voice, screen, classroom, and rule that tells them who they're allowed to be. They're being rewarded for how well they can suppress their truth, override their instincts, and follow the script.

And the younger it starts, the deeper it sinks in.

They're not being taught to *tune in*.
They're being taught to ask permission.
To seek approval.
To doubt their knowing.
To ignore their inner "no."
To colour inside the lines, even when their soul wants to paint the sky purple and draw blue people.

## We Must Help Them Build Awareness Before the World Teaches Them to Forget

Awareness is how we interrupt the programming. It's how we teach our children to notice what they feel, not just what they're told. To pay attention to the quiet voice within, not just the loud voice of authority. To see the difference between *who they are* and *who they've been told to be.*

They are so susceptible. So open. So deeply attuned to the energy around them. And if we don't show them how to stay connected to their own awareness, the world will give them a thousand reasons to disconnect from it.

This chapter is not about how to be a perfect parent. It's not about raising flawless children.

It's about raising *aware* children and keeping them connected to their innate inner intelligence, their intuition.

It's about seeing them, really seeing them, and helping them stay rooted in the truth of who they are. Because when you raise a child in awareness, you're not just shaping their future. You're protecting their soul.

## Children Are Not Blank Slates

Children are not blank slates waiting to be filled; they are whole beings who arrive with their own essence, wisdom, and inner guidance. Our role is not to shape them into who we think they should be, but to help them stay connected to who they already are.

And that begins with us being in awareness.

## Seeing Your Child, Not Just Managing Them

Too often, parenting becomes a cycle of managing behaviour rather than meeting the being. We focus on outcomes, did they eat, sleep, behave, perform, and forget to pause and ask, *who are they in this moment?*

Awareness is what allows us to truly *see* our children.
Not through the lens of our expectations.
Not through the lens of fear.
Not through the lens of society's standards.
But through the lens of *presence*.

It's the difference between reacting to a tantrum and being curious about what the tantrum is trying to say.
Between enforcing quiet and noticing what's been silenced.
Between pushing them to succeed and helping them feel safe to explore.

## Children Learn Awareness by Being Exposed to It

Just like intuition, awareness is *caught* more than taught. Children absorb our presence, our regulation, and our attention, far more than our words.

If we want our children to grow into conscious, emotionally intelligent adults, we must show them what it looks like to be aware.

That means becoming aware of *ourselves* first:

- The tone we use when we're tired
- The stories we project onto their behaviour
- The unresolved fears we carry about their future
- The way we speak to ourselves in their presence

Children are incredibly intuitive. They feel everything, even when they don't have the words. And they often make those feelings *mean something* about themselves.

Your unspoken stress might become *"I'm a burden."*
Your distractedness might become *"I'm not important."*

This isn't about guilt.
It's about *reclaiming* the power of awareness, because the moment we become aware, we have the opportunity to repair. Can you imagine a world where parents take responsibility for their actions and regulate their nervous systems with their children?!

**Awareness Helps You Parent the Soul, Not Just the Surface**

When we lean into awareness, we begin to recognise what's really happening beneath the surface of our children's behaviour. A child who appears to be "acting out" might not be misbehaving at all; they could be overstimulated, emotionally overwhelmed, or simply not feeling understood. A child who "won't listen" might actually be feeling unseen or disconnected, struggling to express what they can't yet put into words. A child who is often labelled as "too sensitive" might, in fact, be deeply intuitive, absorbing more from the world around them than most people realise, and needing support to navigate all that they feel.

With awareness, we stop taking these moments so personally. We stop rushing to label or correct them. Instead, we begin to see them as invitations, not to control, but to connect. We respond with curiosity rather than criticism, presence rather than pressure.

Because when we parent with awareness, we're not just addressing symptoms. We're tending to the soul.

**Intuition in Parenting: Trust What You Know Without Proof**

There will be moments when your intuition knows something that no book or expert can explain.

You'll *feel* that something is off, even when your child says it's fine.
You'll *sense* that your child needs rest instead of discipline.
You'll *know* that a school, teacher, or friend isn't right, even if it doesn't make logical sense.

Trust that.

That is your soul speaking to theirs.

And the more you model this kind of trust, the more your child learns to trust themselves.

**Bringing It Back to the Home**

You don't need perfect routines or ideal circumstances to raise an aware child.
What they need most is *you*. Your attention. Your presence. Your willingness to be wrong, to repair, to grow.

So when you find yourself overwhelmed, come back to this question:

*"Am I seeing my child right now, or am I seeing my story about them?"*

Awareness brings us back to the truth about them and about ourselves.

**Make It Playful.**

Awareness and intuition don't have to be heavy, deep, or serious. With children, the most powerful way to teach these things is through *play*. In fact, play is just as important for us adults too.

That's why I included two very simple but powerful practices in this book: the **Morning Thought Redirect** and the **Traffic Light Game**.

Children love them.
They light up when they get the traffic light game right.
We light up when they remind us how magical it is to tune in.

You can also try the **Parking Game** with your kids. It's one of our favourites.

When you're driving together, invite them to close their eyes and *feel* where you'll find a spot. Will it be on the left or the right? Close to the entrance or further away? Let them tune in and guess, not with logic, but with their body.

They'll surprise you.

And you'll surprise yourself.

Let me share one of our moments...

We were heading to IKEA for a shopping trip, and as we entered the parking area, I suddenly got the nudge to stop. Just like that, no explanation. I didn't see anything, but I trusted it. So I stopped.

Both my daughters looked at me, puzzled. "Mum... there's no parking here."

I just smiled, and said, "I got a hit to stop."

Within seconds, a couple walked down the row and got into their car, parked *right next to us*. I didn't even need to move my car. I simply pulled into their spot.

They were stunned. I wasn't just smiling because I got a good parking spot, but because they got to witness intuition in action.

It's fun. It's practical. It's how we make this real, and when we model it, they begin to trust their own hits, too.

We're not just raising kids to obey rules or follow instructions. We're raising children to trust their bodies. To listen to their inner yes and their quiet no.
To know that life isn't just about logic, it's about listening.

So, play with them. Practice with them.
Talk about your morning thoughts.
Guess the traffic lights together.
Feel into the parking spots.

These little moments become the foundation for a lifetime of self-trust.

Let awareness and intuition be a *shared language* in your home, one that reminds them every day: *you can trust what you know, even when it doesn't make sense yet.*

**Teaching Them to Tune In, Even to Their Bodies**
Another beautiful way to help children trust their inner

guidance is by teaching them to check in when they're not feeling well. Instead of reaching for medicine immediately, we can guide them to ask a simple, powerful question:

"Is this mine?"

Sometimes, what they're feeling isn't physical; it's energetic. Children are deeply intuitive and sensitive to the people around them. They can pick up on stress, pain, or emotions from others without even realising it.

In our home, we've seen this again and again.

If one of the girls gets a headache, and there's no clear reason for it, they'll check in with the rest of us in the house to see who's got the headache, and often, one of us will say, "Yes, I actually do have a headache."

And just like that, they know it wasn't theirs. They felt someone else's discomfort. And because they have that awareness, they don't need to carry the pain. They can simply say, "It's not mine," and let it go.

This is emotional intelligence at its highest form, embodied and intuitive. No charts, no long explanations. Just presence.

And in a home with three women, when one of us is on our period, we often feel each other's pain. We move with empathy. We hold each other with understanding. There's no shame, no hiding, just awareness, compassion, and choice.

Can you imagine what kind of world we'd live in if more people were this connected to themselves and each other?

If instead of suppressing symptoms, we listened to them.
If instead of numbing emotions, we explored them.
If instead of reacting, we paused and chose to respond with awareness.

That world is possible.

And it starts with how we raise our children.

## Teaching Children About Trauma and Projection

One of the greatest gifts we can give our children is the ability to recognise what is theirs and what belongs to someone else.

Because here's the truth: we all carry trauma. And unless we become aware of it, we pass it on.

When someone hasn't processed their own emotional pain, it often leaks out as control, blame, jealousy, or manipulation. It can show up in friendships, family dynamics, school environments, and later, romantic relationships. And when children don't understand what projection is, they often internalise it. They think they're the problem—that they're too much, not enough, that something is wrong with them.

But when we teach them about trauma, not as something shameful, but as something that everyone carries in different ways, we empower them to see clearly. To hold compassion without carrying the weight of someone else's wounds. To discern between empathy and self-abandonment.

Let me show you what this looks like in real life.

**Febe's Story: Awareness in Teenage Relationships**

My eldest daughter, Febe, had her first long-term relationship at 16. She really liked this boy, we'll call him Adam. Over time, his behaviour started showing red flags. He became increasingly controlling. He wanted to know where she was at all times. He was jealous and emotionally reactive. She didn't have the freedom to meet with friends or take a day for herself.

It wasn't that he was "a bad person." Adam had experienced trauma in his own life. His mother had suffered abuse in her marriage to his father. Adam also experienced abuse from his dad. That unprocessed trauma shaped the way Adam related to love. Control became his way of seeking safety, and Febe recognised it. She saw the pattern, and with so much emotional maturity for her age, she tried to help him see it too. But he wasn't ready. He couldn't yet take responsibility for what was his, and the weight of that started falling on her.

Eventually, Febe made one of the hardest choices a young girl can make, she ended the relationship. Not because she didn't care, but because she cared enough about herself to walk away.

That is awareness in action.

That is what it looks like when we raise children who can recognise the difference between love and attachment, between empathy and enabling.

**Chloe's Story: Friendship and Self-Respect**

My youngest daughter, Chloe, had her own moment of awareness much earlier. She was about ten years old when she started pulling away from her friend across the street, let's call her Izzy.

They had been close for years, playing every day, sharing secrets, growing up together. But something shifted. Chloe no longer wanted to go over as often. I didn't push. I simply noticed, and one afternoon, I asked Chloe what was wrong when she didn't want to play.

She said quietly but clearly, "Izzy always wants to be the boss. She never lets me choose. She wants things her way all the time." Chloe didn't feel free in that friendship anymore.

I could see she had already come to her own conclusion, and she was right. Her boundaries were being crossed. She wasn't having fun anymore. And one day, she simply said, "I'm done. I don't want to be friends with her anymore."

She didn't make it dramatic. She just listened to what didn't feel right and honoured that feeling.

This is what awareness does. It gives our children the ability to listen to themselves, to recognise the subtle shifts in their energy, and to know when something isn't good for them anymore, even if it used to be. It gives them power over themselves and their lives.

**Awareness and Intuition: The Compass for a Fulfilling Life**

Imagine a world where children grow up knowing how to listen to themselves.
Not just to the rules. Not just to what's expected.
But to *their truth*.

This is what awareness and intuition makes possible.

When we teach our children to be aware of what they feel, what they notice, and what doesn't feel right in their bodies, we're giving them a compass—not just for survival but for fulfilment, joy, and purpose.

And when we teach them to trust the subtle nudges, that feeling in their gut, the sense that something's off, or the quiet knowing that says, "this is right for me", we are guiding them to live in alignment with their soul.

They begin to choose differently:

- They choose friends who respect their boundaries.
- They walk away from relationships that don't honour

their heart.
- They choose careers that match their values, not just their resume.
- They don't ignore the whisper that says, "I want something more", they follow it.

This doesn't mean life will always be easy or perfect. But it means they will have the tools to navigate it. To come back to themselves. To discern their own path, even when the world is loud.

Most people spend decades trying to unlearn the programming they inherited in childhood.
But what if we raised children who didn't have to forget who they were in the first place?

What if we raised children who knew, from the start, that their awareness was valid, and their intuition was trustworthy?

That is the revolution.
And it starts with us.

**Shaping Soul-Led Rebels**

When we raise kids with awareness and intuition, we're not just shaping good humans, we're shaping a better world.

A world where people trust themselves.
Where children grow into adults who can hold space for others

without abandoning themselves.

Where love and compassion are normal, not rare.

Where power doesn't come from control, but from connection.

So, keep playing the games.

Keep having the conversations.

Keep asking the questions.

Because this is how the revolution begins, not with big grand gestures, but with everyday moments. With a parent who chooses to teach their child that they are powerful, intuitive, and deeply wise.

**In This Chapter, We Explored…**

• How the world is conditioning our children to seek approval, suppress their truth, and disconnect from their inner guidance.
• Why awareness is essential for helping children stay connected to who they truly are.
• The difference between parenting behaviour and parenting the soul.
• How trauma and projection can show up in relationships, and how awareness helps our children navigate these patterns.
• The power of teaching children to recognise what's theirs and what they've picked up from others.
• Playful and practical ways to nurture awareness and intuition at home, including the Morning Thought exercise, the Traffic Light Game, and the Parking Game.
• How to support your child in tuning into their body and energy when they feel unwell.
• The vision of a new kind of world, one where our children grow up in tune with themselves, each other, and their inner power.

.

## CHAPTER 10

## AWAKENING ABUNDANCE

> *"Awareness is the root of abundance. You can only receive what you're awake enough to notice."*
> *- Unknown*

**Awakening Abundance (Manifesting)**

Most people think manifesting is about *getting* what you want. The car. The money. The partner. The dream home. And while there's nothing wrong with those desires, the way the world teaches manifesting often leaves people chasing something just out of reach, like abundance is something external they need to attract, rather than something internal they need to awaken or align too.

The truth is that every person on this planet is already manifesting. It's not a special skill or secret formula; it's a natural byproduct of being alive. But most people are manifesting unconsciously or aligning with their negative habits and limiting beliefs. They're doing it from a lack of awareness, from the same old beliefs, fears, and patterns they've carried since childhood. When you live on autopilot, you're manifesting by default, from your conditioning, not your consciousness and that's often the real problem when they try to manifest and fail. Without awareness, you're not creating something new; you're recycling what's familiar.

You may be visualising a new reality, but if you're still anchored in old pain, scarcity, and stories of unworthiness, nothing truly changes.
You may say the affirmations and make the vision board, but if you haven't cleared the static within, you'll miss the deeper cues and callings that are trying to guide you.

Most people are manifesting from their *wounds*, not their *wisdom*. They're calling in more of what they're trying to escape.

That's why awareness is everything.
Until you become aware of what's really running the show—your subconscious patterns, emotional triggers, and inherited fears—you'll keep manifesting the same life with different packaging. It's like trying to plant a garden on concrete.
The seeds may be beautiful. The intention might be strong. But the ground isn't ready.

Awakening abundance isn't about adding more to yourself. It's about stripping back the layers of doubt, pressure, and programming that told you you weren't enough. It's about noticing the cracks in the old record you've been playing and choosing to write a new one. It's a return, not a chase. A remembering, not a reaching.

Because true manifesting doesn't come from effort, it comes from awareness and alignment.

Your job isn't to force or fake it.
Your job is to *see clearly* what's going on within you and *trust the intuitive nudges* that begin to rise as a result.

This is where awareness and intuition, your two spirit senses, become essential. They are the bridge between the seen and the unseen. The compass pointing you back to what's already yours.

Where force fails, flow begins.
And that's when abundance awakens.

> *"The key to abundance is meeting limited circumstances with unlimited awareness."*
> *- Marianne Williamson*

**First, Let's Get Clear on What Alignment Is**
Alignment is a word that is often used in spiritual and manifesting circles, but is often unclear as to what it is.

So, let's ground it in something real.

Being in alignment simply means being aware of yourself, and your actions are guided by your inner guidance.
It's not about getting everything right.
It's not about being high-vibe all the time.
It's about being honest with what's happening inside of you, and choosing to move in a way that honours your truth.

By now, you know that everything we've been working with, awareness and intuition, isn't just theory. It's a way of living. And *this* is what alignment actually looks like in practice:
You notice what's happening within you.
You listen to what feels right.
And you take the next step from that place.

It might not make sense to anyone else.
It might not even make sense to your logical mind.
But it *feels right*. It feels peaceful. It feels clear in your body.
And that's what alignment is.

It's not about having all the answers.
It's about being present enough to recognise when you've drifted from your truth, and choosing to return to it.

Yes, you'll fall out of alignment sometimes. You're human.
But the beauty is, you'll notice it faster. You'll feel the tension, the friction, the misalignment. And instead of spiralling, you'll pause, recenter, and realign.

> *"You're not here to push your way forward. You're here to align with what's already calling you."*
> *- Leonie du Toit*

So, as we step into this next layer of manifesting, keep this at the centre:
Alignment is not the result of the manifestation; it's the entry point.
And when you begin from alignment, the unfolding becomes so much more natural, soulful, and powerful.

**The Role of Choice in Manifesting**

Once you understand what alignment really is—awareness and intuition working together—the next piece becomes clear: **choice**.

Manifesting isn't magic.
It's not just about calling things in.
It's about **choosing** to walk toward the version of you who already has what you desire.

That choice happens in every moment.

Every thought you think.
Every word you speak.
Every action you take.

It's all either reinforcing the old story... or aligning you with a new one.

And this is where awareness is non-negotiable.
Because without awareness, you won't even *see* the choice.
You'll just run on autopilot, repeating the same reactions, the same fears, the same habits, and wondering why nothing changes.

But when you're awake to yourself...
When you can pause and notice what's happening inside you...
You create space to choose differently.

You choose to breathe instead of lashing out.
You choose to hold the vision instead of spiralling into doubt.
You choose to take a small step forward, even when it feels scary.

That's manifestation in motion.

It's not always grand or dramatic.
It's subtle. Quiet. Moment by moment.

You don't manifest a new life by waiting for a lightning bolt or chanting the perfect affirmation.
You manifest it by making one aligned choice at a time.

When you choose with awareness and follow the nudge of your intuition, you shift your frequency.
You begin living in resonance with what you've been asking

for and that's when the universe can respond.

> *"In every moment, you are either creating from your conditioning or your consciousness. One leads to repetition. The other leads to transformation."*
> *- Leonie du Toit*

So, the next time you wonder why your manifestations aren't landing, come back to this:

**What are you choosing?**
And are those choices rooted in awareness… or old stories?

This is the bridge.
This is the path.
This is how we manifest with clarity, purpose, and power.

### How to Make Aligned Choices (Clarity Is Key)

Alignment isn't a feeling you chase; it's a way of moving through life. And the way you move is shaped by the choices you make.

But here's the thing:
*You can't make aligned choices if you're unclear about what you want.*

When your energy is vague, the universe responds vaguely. When your intention is scattered, so are your results. It's like walking into a restaurant and saying, "I'll have… food." They could bring you anything, cold soup, a plate of toast, something you didn't want or even like. But when you say, "I'll have the grilled chicken, no onions, extra avocado, lemon on the side," you're far more likely to receive exactly what you asked for.

Manifesting works the same way. The clearer you are about what you desire, and the more honest you are about why you want it, the easier it becomes to recognise the steps that align with it.

Clarity creates direction.
Awareness reveals your options.
Intuition guides your next step.

When these three work together, every choice you make becomes a declaration of alignment.

So if you feel stuck or uncertain… pause.
Ask yourself:

- What do I actually want here?
- What would the aligned version of me choose?
- What feels true in my body right now?

> *"You don't get what you want. You get what you choose, over and over again."*
> *- Leonie du Toit*

Let's take this deeper.

Being specific is one of the most important parts of this process.

Let's say you want a car. If you say, "One for about $20K," you've just opened yourself up to thousands of possibilities. But if you get crystal clear, make, model, year, colour, trim, tinted windows, roof rack, sound system, leather seats, you create a very specific signal.

Go sit in that car. Go for a test drive. Smell the interior. Feel the steering wheel. Get to know it as if it were your own right now.

And then? Visualise from that place.

Not from *wanting*, but from *having*.

See the car in your driveway.

See yourself running errands, picking up the kids, washing it outside your home, and putting fuel in it.

See yourself *living it*.

What's going to happen is that the universe will begin to present opportunities, send you more clients, you'll receive unexpected money, and abundance will start flowing in. But here's the catch: you need **awareness** to see those opportunities, and **intuition** to know which ones to follow.

This is where alignment becomes real.

You don't just visualise, you respond.

You co-create.

You stay open and awake to what's moving toward you and what's being asked of you in return.

And as you begin getting clear on *what* you want, there's something else to remember…

**You don't want money for the sake of money.**
**You want it for the feeling you believe it will give you.**

You want the car to feel confident.
You want the holiday to feel free.
You want the house to feel grounded, proud, and at peace.
You want success to feel enough.

Every desire you have is pointing you toward a state of being.
A frequency.
A feeling.

And if you miss that and stay fixated on the object, you might get the thing but still feel empty.
Because the manifestation was never really about the *thing*.
It was about the *experience* you were craving underneath it.

This is where awareness transforms everything.
When you tune into what you truly desire, not just on the surface, but beneath it, you stop chasing and start aligning.

You begin to ask:
What do I really want to feel?
And what choices, thoughts, and energies will help me feel that now?

That's the access point to true abundance.
Not later. Not "once it arrives."
But right here. Right now.

> *"You think you want the thing. But what you really want is the feeling you believe the thing will give you."*
> *- Leonie du Toit*

The beauty is that once you begin living in that frequency, the thing itself often shows up with ease.
Not because you forced it.
But because you finally matched it.

### A Note on Clarity: Watch for Competing or Diluted Desires

Sometimes you *think* you're clear, but your energy is split.
You say you want abundance, but deep down, you're afraid of being seen.
You ask for love, but you're still guarded from being hurt.
You want growth, but you're clinging to comfort.

These are called competing desires, and they dilute your manifesting power.
Awareness helps you catch them.
Pay attention to where you feel pulled in two directions.

Use your intuition to sense what's real and what's protective programming.

When you get honest about your *true* desires and stop sending mixed signals to the universe, you create a clear, magnetic frequency that calls in what's meant for you.

**Consistency**

Manifesting isn't about doing it perfectly every day. It's about showing up with intention, even when things feel messy or uncertain.

There will be days when your energy dips.
There will be times when you question it all.
That doesn't mean it's not working. That doesn't mean you've failed.

When you get tired, don't give up, rest.
Breathe. Reconnect. Regroup. And then keep going.

Some days you'll move mountains. Other days, it might just be one small step.
Some days, the step might look like pausing or even stepping back, not in defeat but to see a new way forward.

Consistency isn't about speed.
It's about staying *in relationship* with your desires.
It's about keeping the channel open.
And it's about trusting that even the smallest aligned action still

sends a signal to the universe:
I'm showing up. I'm available. I'm ready.

**Letting Go of the "How?"**

One of the biggest traps in manifesting is getting caught up in the *how*.

How is this going to happen?
How will the money come?
How will I meet the right person?
How is this even possible?

Your mind will search for a plan, a timeline, a shortcut. But manifesting doesn't work like that. And honestly, it's not your job to figure it out.

Your job is to get clear on the *what* and the *why*.
What do you truly desire?
Why does it matter to you?

Then, you align, you take the steps, and you stay open. The *how* is not up to you. That's the domain of the universe.

The universe doesn't deliver in a straight line.
It delivers through people.
Through conversations.
Through sudden ideas.
Through a post you stumble across.

Through a detour that leads to a door you never even knew existed.

But if you're obsessed with controlling the how, you'll miss all of that.
You'll walk right past the opportunity because it doesn't look the way you expected it to.

Imagine a little child playing with his toy car. He pushes it too hard, and one of the wheels comes off. No matter how hard he tries, he can't fix it. Frustrated, he walks over to his dad, holds up the broken toy and says, "Help."

His dad smiles, gently takes the car from his hands, and examines it to see how he can fix it. But the child, impatient and frustrated that his dad isn't fixing it fast enough, snatches it back and tries again on his own.

His dad doesn't stop him. He knows his son needs to learn. So, he sits back and watches patiently.

The child wrestles with the toy again, growing even more frustrated. Eventually, he passes it back to his dad, and again he says, "Help."
Once more, his dad begins to work on it.
The child watches... then suddenly grabs it again, "I know how!", and goes back to struggling.

Still, his dad waits.
He can see his child is struggling, but he doesn't interrupt,

because he knows that unless the child chooses to surrender, he won't really be able to receive the help he needs.

Finally, the boy hands the car back to his dad again, this time in tears.
No words, just surrender.
His father takes the toy, quietly clicks the wheel back into place in just a few seconds, and hands it back.
The boy wipes his tears, takes the car, and walks away, peaceful again.

This is how so many of us interact with God or the Universe when we're trying to manifest something.

We ask for help.
We say we're letting go of the outcome.
We offer it up in prayer.

But then... we grab it right back.
We replay it in our minds, worrying, doubting, trying to figure it out ourselves.
We ask again, "Help."
And then once more, we interfere, mentally, emotionally, energetically, trying to make it happen on our own timeline.

But the Universe is patient.
God is patient.
And because we have free will, He will not force His way in.
He will wait, lovingly, quietly, until we're truly ready to let go and place it entirely in His hands.

And when we finally do?
When we surrender completely, without trying to control or direct the process,
That's when the solution arrives with ease.

Sometimes in seconds.
Sometimes in ways we couldn't have imagined.
But always with perfect timing.

> *"Surrender to what is. Let go of what was.*
> *Have faith in what will be."*
> *- Sonia Ricotti*

This is also where impatience becomes a massive spiritual block. We want things now. We want certainty. We want evidence. But we forget: there are energies that have to fall into place first. There are things shifting behind the scenes that you can't always see.

Most importantly, the time it takes for your manifestation to arrive is often the exact time needed for your own healing.
It's the space where you become who you need to be in order to receive what you've asked for.
It's where the deeper work happens, the identity shifts, the emotional clearing, the expansion of your capacity to hold more.

Surrender isn't giving up, it's *giving over*.
It's trusting that once you've done your part, life will meet you halfway.
Sometimes in ways that feel miraculous.
Sometimes in ways that only make sense after the fact.

And I've experienced this firsthand...

But before I tell you my story, go back five lines where I said, "Surrender isn't giving up, it's giving over." Did you perhaps notice your stomach turn? Did it feel tight in your chest just thinking of how you can't give over, never…you have to keep control of it all? I know my stomach turned when I read this for myself while doing the editing for the manuscript. Clearly there is a layer of control presenting itself to me that needs to be looked at. Can you see how awareness shows us where our blocks and limiting beliefs are?

Ok, back to my story.

In 2017, shortly after I ended my marriage, I found myself in a season of financial hardship. I had my two small girls to look after, and my business wasn't in a position to cover all of our expenses. I was doing my best, but I was struggling.

I prayed. I asked the Universe for help. I trusted that it would come,
I just didn't know how.

I couldn't see a way forward.
I surrendered...

A few days later, my ex-mother-in-law unexpectedly called to ask how the girls and I were doing. Not being one to complain, I told her we were well but that things were a little tight. I didn't let her know just how much I was struggling.

What she said next brought me to tears.
She told me that during her morning meditation, she had received a message from her guides to deposit a thousand dollars into my account.

I cried.
Not just because of the money, but because I didn't expect the mother of the man I had just left to be the one who would help me in such a generous and spirit-led way.

This is one of those moments that reminded me why we have to **let go of the how**.
Our job is not to figure it all out.
Our job is to ask, to align, and to trust that the support will come, often in ways we never could have imagined.

That memory also brings me back to another moment. I was sitting in meditation, praying for money to come in. I was overwhelmed. I needed so much for so many different things, and I didn't even know how to ask clearly.

I remember saying,

*"I don't know how to be specific about what I want. There's so much I need it for. If I could just receive a large sum of money, then I'll figure it out myself."*

And in that quiet space, I heard it, clear and undeniable:
*"But what if God has something so much better in store for you? What if a large sum of money will not make up all the gifts and abundance that the Universe has in store for you?"*

That shifted everything in me.

Trust is one of the hardest things we're asked to do on this path, but it's also one of the most satisfying and sacred.

When we truly surrender the *how*, we open ourselves to *who* and *what* can be used to bless us. We begin to understand that the Universe doesn't work in straight lines; it works in miracles.

This is where both awareness and intuition come alive. You need to be aware enough to see the signs and intuitive enough to follow them, even when they don't look like the plan.

Let go of the timeline.
Let go of the script.
Let go of how it's *supposed* to happen.

Stay connected to the desire.
Stay present in the process.
And trust that the how will always reveal itself when you're in

alignment with the what.

> *"Faith is taking the first step even when you don't see the whole staircase."*
> - Martin Luther King Jr.

**Trusting What You Can't Yet See**

Manifesting rarely follows a straight, logical path. More often than not, it challenges your expectations, stretches your faith, and asks you to move before you can see the full picture.

That's why **trust** is such a vital part of the process.

It's easy to trust when things are going your way, when the path is clear, when the signs are obvious, and when everything falls neatly into place.
But the real invitation is to trust when the thing that shows up doesn't look like what you expected… or when the choice in front of you makes no sense to your logical mind.

Imagine this:

You've set a clear intention to call in a new job, one that offers more purpose, better balance, space to grow, and yes, more abundance. Soon, two offers arrive. One pays significantly more. It looks impressive on paper.
The other pays less, but something about it feels right. There's

a sense of ease. Groundedness. A quiet knowing in your body that says, *this is the one.*

Your mind might immediately go into overdrive.
*"Go for the money. Be practical. This is the smart choice."*
But something deeper whispers, *"Choose the other one."*

If you're in awareness, you'll notice the difference in how each option feels in your body. One may feel tight and forced, even if it looks good externally. The other might bring a sense of peace, expansion, and resonance, even if it's less flashy.

You choose to trust the nudge.
You follow what feels aligned, even if it doesn't make sense just yet.

And then, weeks later, it all becomes clear.
That "lesser" offer turns out to be the very thing you were manifesting all along, just in a form you didn't recognise at first.
The culture is nourishing.
The leadership sees and values your potential.
There's room for growth, purpose, creativity, and in time, the financial abundance follows, too.

This is what it means to manifest from alignment, not ego.
To let your soul, not your spreadsheet, lead the way.

> *"Trust isn't just believing it will happen. It's being willing to follow the path even when it doesn't look like the one you had in mind."*
> *-Leonie du Toit*

Manifesting from this place doesn't always guarantee comfort, but it does guarantee truth.

And when you choose truth, you open yourself to receive what you actually asked for, even if it looks different from what you imagined.

Sometimes, the path to your manifestation doesn't appear until you take the step.

Sometimes, the thing you desire shows up wrapped in unfamiliar packaging.

And sometimes, your soul leads you to something far better than what your mind would have settled for.

That's the power of trust.

Not passive waiting, but courageous movement in the direction of what feels true.

And in that movement, everything you've asked for is already waiting.

## The Clearing Comes with the Calling

Here's another truth about manifesting that's often left out:

When you call in something new, what no longer fits will begin to fall away.

This isn't a glitch in the system.
It's part of the process.

When you ask for more love, old relationship wounds may surface.
When you ask for wealth, you might be confronted with your beliefs about worth.
When you ask for expansion, you may feel your fears tightening their grip.

It's not because you're doing it wrong.
It's because you're being prepared to receive what you're asking for.

Think of it like cleaning out your closet. You want to buy new clothes, but your wardrobe is stuffed with things that no longer fit, no longer feel good, or never really suited you in the first place. So, before the new can come in, the old has to go.

The same happens internally.

You may find yourself shedding identities, roles, habits, and even relationships.
You may bump up against fear, resistance, doubt, or discomfort.

But if you stay aware, you'll see it for what it is:
Clearing. Making space. Creating room for what you actually desire.

Let's say you're calling in a healthy, aligned relationship. You meet someone who seems perfect, but as things progress, your old fear of abandonment resurfaces. Instead of shutting down or running, you choose to stay present. You breathe. You feel. You become aware of the story, and you choose not to let it drive your actions. That clearing moment is just as much a part of the manifestation as the person showing up.

> *"Manifesting isn't just about calling it in. It's about becoming someone who can hold it when it arrives."*
> *- Leonie du Toit*

This is the deep work.
And this is why awareness and intuition are not optional in the manifesting process.
They are the tools that guide you through the clearing, help you stay in trust, and prepare you to receive what you've asked for.

### The Power of Gratitude in Manifesting

Gratitude plays a bigger role in manifesting than most people realise. At its core, gratitude is an energetic signal that you've received something.

Think about it, how do you know when someone has accepted a gift? They say thank you.

Gratitude is the natural response to receiving.
It's the closure of the loop. The final step that says, *"I've received this, and I recognise the value of it."*

And here's the key:

When you embody gratitude now, you begin to align with the frequency of having.
Not wanting.
Not hoping.
*Having.*

This is why gratitude is so powerful in the manifesting process.
It shifts you out of lack and into presence.
It helps you embody the energy of "it's already done."
And from that place, you become magnetic to more.

When you're grateful, you're not trying to get.
You're acknowledging that something has already arrived or is on its way.
You're tuning your energy to the truth that you are supported, provided for, and connected to something greater.

So, whether you're holding the thing in your hand or holding it in your heart, gratitude is a powerful activator.
It's not just a nice emotion. It's a *manifesting posture*.

Gratitude says to the universe:
"I see what's already here. And I'm available for more."

**The Gratitude Trap**

While gratitude is powerful, there's a subtle trap that many people fall into, especially when they're trying to manifest something they *really* want or need. I call it **the gratitude trap**.

It's what happens when we confuse gratitude with relief.

And I know this one personally.

There was a time when I was in a season of lack. Money was tight, and I had been holding out hope for a client payment to come through. When it finally landed, I did what I always do: I put my hand on my heart to say thank you.

But this time, something felt off.

As I dropped into my body, I realised that it wasn't gratitude. It was relief.

I wasn't grounded in the energy of receiving, and I wasn't only grateful. I was relieved that the pressure had lifted, and that moment was a turning point for me.

Because here's the difference:
Relief is about escape. Gratitude is about embodiment.

Relief says, *"Thank goodness that's over."*
Gratitude says, *"I see what's here, and I honour it."*

Relief often shows up when we've been manifesting from survival energy.
From stress. From fear. From urgency.
It's not wrong, it's human. But it's not the frequency that draws in aligned, sustainable abundance.

Gratitude, on the other hand, is grounded.
It's present.
It's powerful because it says: *"Even here, I see the good. Even now, I trust what's unfolding."*

If we're not aware, we can fall into the trap of calling relief gratitude, thinking we're in an energy of receiving when we're actually still bracing for the next struggle.

This is why **awareness is everything**.

It allows you to pause and ask:
*What am I really feeling right now?*
*Am I anchored in trust... or just grateful that the discomfort stopped?*

There's no shame in relief.
But don't stop there.
Let relief open the door, and then walk through it into real, embodied gratitude.

The more you practice this level of self-honesty, the more magnetic you become. Not because you're trying to manifest faster, but because you're finally resonating with the truth of *having* instead of *needing*.

**What to Do When You Feel Stuck**

Let's be honest, sometimes you just feel stuck.
You know what you want. You're trying to align. You're doing "the work."
But emotionally, mentally, or energetically… You feel heavy.
Flat.
Disconnected.
And no amount of visualising or positive thinking seems to shift it.

That's normal. And it's okay.
We all hit moments like this.
The key is not to fight the stuckness but to *move with it* until it starts to loosen.

Here are some simple, real-world ways to shift your state and reconnect to your power:

**1. Change your environment.**

Stuck energy often loops in the same space.
Step outside. Open a window. Take a walk.
Go to the beach, the forest, your garden, anywhere that gives your body and energy system a new experience.

**2. Move your body.**

Movement clears stagnation.
Dance in your living room. Shake it out. Stretch. Do a few yoga poses.
Even a few deep breaths with your arms overhead can break through emotional heaviness.

**3. Do something small but productive.**

Clean one drawer. Wash the dishes. Water your plants.
The goal isn't perfection, it's motion. Small wins re-establish a sense of agency, and that's what begins to shift your state.

**4. Speak out loud.**

Talk to your guides, to God, to yourself. Say how you feel.
Speak your stuck-ness into the space and invite support.
Let the words move the energy.

**5. Use the "one better thought" practice.**

If you're spiralling in negative thoughts, don't try to leap to joy.
Just ask, *"What's one better thought I can reach for right now?"*
You're not trying to jump from despair to bliss, you're just reaching for *better*, not perfect.

**6. Do one thing that brings you into the present.**

Pet your dog. Drink a glass of water slowly. Stand in the sun. Presence brings peace, and peace is fertile ground for intuitive guidance.

**7. Ask your awareness one question.**

Instead of forcing your way forward, get curious.
Ask, *"What am I not seeing right now?"*
Or *"What's one thing I could shift, just a little, to support myself today?"*
Let your intuition respond.

> *"Stuck isn't a place, it's a signal. It's an invitation to pause, shift, soften, and listen."*
> *-Leonie du Toit*

Remember: your job isn't to feel amazing all the time.
Your job is to notice when you've disconnected and gently come back.
Not with pressure. But with presence. The more you do this, the more moments of alignment you'll have.

These tiny shifts don't just help you feel better. They help you *remember who you are*.
And from there… the next aligned step becomes clear.

**In This Chapter, We Explored...**

Manifesting isn't just about calling in what you want, it's about awakening to what's already available when you're aligned.

We unpacked the difference between chasing desires from a place of fear or programming, and consciously creating from awareness and intuition, the spirit senses that guide every step of your manifesting journey.

We looked at what alignment really means, how clarity influences your results, and why specificity is a powerful signal to the universe. We explored how manifesting is less about the "thing" and more about the *feeling* you're trying to experience, and how you can begin to feel that now, not later.

We touched on:

- How to make aligned choices through clarity.
- The importance of trust (especially when it makes no logical sense).
- How to let go of the "how" and surrender the outcome
- Why consistency, gratitude, and healing are essential to receiving.
- And what to do when you feel stuck or low, because even that is part of the journey.

## CHAPTER 11

## AWARENESS IN EVERYDAY LIFE

**Awareness in Everyday Life**

Spirituality isn't something we only do on the mat, in meditation, or on retreat. It's who we are when no one is watching. It's how we show up in the small, ordinary moments, when the kids are yelling, when the coffee spills, when you're stuck in traffic, when your plans fall apart, or when your partner says something that stings.

This is where awareness matters most.

It's easy to feel calm and wise when things are quiet and flowing, but real transformation happens in the everyday. In the uncomfortable. In the reactive. In the messy middle of life.

Awareness isn't about avoiding these moments. It's about noticing what's happening *within* you when these moments arise.

- What thought just played out in your mind?

- What belief got triggered?
- What story did you start telling yourself?
- What habitual reaction is trying to take over?

Awareness gives you that tiny window to pause. To interrupt the autopilot. To choose something different.

This is the training ground.

**In the supermarket line, when someone cuts in front of you.**
Do you get irritated, or can you take a breath and feel your feet on the ground?

**In conversation.**
Do you listen with presence, or are you preparing your next response?

**With your children.**
Are you parenting from awareness, or repeating the same patterns you grew up with?

Every moment becomes a mirror, an invitation to come back to yourself.

> *"Awareness is not reserved for quiet moments and meditation cushions. It's how you meet your child's frustration, answer the phone, or breathe through a traffic jam. That's where the real work happens."*
> *-Anonymous*

Awareness doesn't remove the need for action. It transforms the *quality* of your action. You're no longer driven by unconscious programming. You're responding, not reacting. You're rooted, not scattered. You're present, not performing.

The more you practice awareness in the little things, the more natural it becomes in the big stuff.

It's not about being perfect. It's about being awake.

And the more awake you are, the more grace, ease, and alignment flow into your life, without needing to chase it.

But don't just take my word for it.

Awareness and intuition are not lofty ideals. They're deeply practical tools that change how people *actually* live, parent, work, love, and make decisions, every single day.

Over the next few pages, I want to share some real-life stories from clients and students who began practising this work in their own lives. You'll see how simple awareness shifts and intuitive nudges led to powerful breakthroughs, not because they followed some perfect formula, but because they were willing to pause, listen, and respond differently.

These stories are here to show you what's possible. To remind you that you're not alone. And to help you recognise that your ordinary life is already filled with sacred moments... if you're aware enough to notice them.

**Client Story: Kara-Lee - The Power of the Pause and the Quiet Yes**

I used to overthink everything. Decisions felt heavy, conversations felt loaded, and I often absorbed the moods and energy of the people around me without even realising it. But awareness and intuition have completely changed the way I move through everyday life.

One summer afternoon, I was standing in the kitchen when I heard the front door open, my partner had just come home from work. As I looked over at him, I instantly picked up on the energy he brought with him: frustration, annoyance, and tension. In the past, I would have unconsciously slipped into that mood too, reacting or shrinking, trying to make things better, or taking it personally. But that day was different.

I noticed the shift. I *became aware* that this wasn't mine to carry. There was a sturdiness in me, a calmness that held steady. My intuition whispered, "Just stay present." So I did. I let him be in his process without making it mine. I listened, stayed grounded, and within minutes, he began lifting out of his funk. That moment changed everything. I saw how awareness gives me space, and intuition gives me direction.

That same inner guidance showed up when I first decided to join Leonie's 12-week Soul Guidance Program(Now TLC Program). At the time, I was stuck, mentally, emotionally, and energetically. Making decisions took forever. I would spend days, sometimes weeks, agonising over every step. But after looking at all the options, I finally said yes. I paid. And the sense of calm and relief that washed over me was instant and undeniable. I became *aware* that when a decision is right for me, when it's aligned, it feels easy. Light. Peaceful. That one choice sparked a series of intuitive decisions that followed, each one helping me trust myself more.

By December 2023, something unexpected happened in a coaching session: I realised I wanted to become a coach myself. The thought had been circling for a while, but in that moment, I could finally hear it clearly. My awareness caught the nudge. My intuition confirmed it.

I started exploring training programs and had an initial conversation with a coaching school. It looked fine on paper, but something felt off. Instead of pushing through, I trusted the feeling; it wasn't a hard no, but it wasn't a yes either. I let it sit. I talked to friends. I explored more. A few conversations later, I found the perfect fit. I enrolled in the right course and even signed my first client soon after.

That experience taught me something powerful: sometimes, "no" doesn't mean stop, it just means pause, or not yet. Awareness helped me notice the difference. Intuition helped me wait for the yes that was truly meant for me.

Today, I live and lead from that place. Not perfectly, but with much more ease. Awareness gives me space to observe.

Intuition gives me the courage to act. Together, they've shifted the way I parent, relate, work, and make decisions, not just in the big moments, but in the quiet, everyday ones too.

## Client Story: Vishna - When the Inner Voice Becomes a Way of Life

There was a time in my life when I moved through the world more with logic than with inner knowing. I thought if I could think my way through things, I'd be safe. I'd be right. I'd be in control. But everything shifted when I signed up to work with Leonie in her 12 week TLC Program. What began as simple curiosity unfolded into a deep transformation. I wasn't just learning new concepts, I was becoming a new person, because Leonie helped me get in touch with my awareness and intuition.

Intuition became my constant companion. A quiet yet powerful friend who now walks with me every day. It whispers in still moments, nudges me during conversations, and guides me in ways I never imagined possible. My awareness, too, sharpened. I began noticing subtle shifts in energy, in spaces, in people, and I could sense what was unspoken but deeply felt. The world started speaking to me in a language beyond words.

This shift didn't just affect my personal life , it changed my professional work as an energy healer. I remember one session that stands out clearly. I was working with a client, fully present and focused on her healing, when I suddenly received a message. But it wasn't for her, it was about her siblings. It didn't make logical sense, and I hesitated. That old part of me wanted proof, certainty, validation. But something deeper in me knew.

I trusted the message and gently shared it with her.

To my surprise, she returned later, amazed. She confirmed everything I had said, things I couldn't have possibly known. That moment was a turning point. It reminded me that healing doesn't just follow a structure. It flows. It reaches into the unseen. And when we have the awareness to receive and the courage to speak, we can become powerful vessels for transformation.

Today, intuition isn't just a tool I use. It's part of who I am. It infuses my work, my relationships, my choices, all of it. And I truly believe that when we open our hearts to listen within, we awaken a deeper intelligence that always knows the way.

**Client Story: Sarah - Letting Go, Leaning In**
(Names Changed)

Earlier in the week, something shifted in me.

For months, I had been carrying the emotional weight of my partner Ross's financial separation from his ex. I was always the one asking questions, reminding him to follow through, gently (and sometimes not so gently) nudging him to take the next step. It had started to feel like nagging, and worse, I could feel resentment beginning to build in my body. It was exhausting.

Then one morning, in the quiet of my own inner space, I heard it, not a dramatic declaration, not a fight, just a soft but certain voice inside that said, *"I'm done pushing."* There was no anger in it. Just peace.

That moment felt like a release. I realised that if Ross truly wanted a future with me, he would take action without needing me to orchestrate it. I didn't have to carry the process anymore. So, I let go. I didn't bring it up again. I didn't drop hints or check in. I simply stepped back, with love.

The very next day, without a word from me, Ross called. He told me that he and his ex had finally set a date to go through everything and formally sort out the separation. Unprompted. On his own.

Later that week, I shared the whole thing with my dear friend Leonie on one of our early morning walks. As I told her about the moment I let go and the surprising call that followed, she smiled and gently reflected something I hadn't fully seen yet: *"That's awareness,"* she said. *"That's your intuition at work."*

She was right.

I had thought I'd just reached my limit. But looking back, I know it was something much deeper. It was my awareness that recognised the cycle I was stuck in. It was my intuition that reminded me to trust, to stop doing and start listening.

I didn't need to push anymore. I needed to let go.
And that one quiet decision changed everything.

**Client Story: Nicky - The Dream That Sealed the Deal**

We had just found the perfect house. Everything about it felt right: the layout, the energy, the location. We made our initial offer and went to bed that night feeling hopeful.

But then I had a dream.

In it, I found myself in a dark alley with the real estate agent and the owner of the house. We were in the middle of a tense negotiation. I told them our offer, and they shook their heads. "It's not enough," they said. They turned and walked away.

In the dream, I didn't chase them. I simply turned and walked in the opposite direction, calm but firm. As I rounded the corner, I heard them call me back. They changed their minds and came back to me, agreeing to the offer.

When I woke up the next morning, the message was crystal clear. I had been shown exactly how to handle the negotiation. I told my husband, "This is what's going to happen. We stick to our offer, not a cent more." He trusted my intuition and agreed.

Later that day, the agent called. Just like in the dream, she said the owner wouldn't accept our offer unless we increased it by $30,000. We calmly said no. We held our ground.

Thirty minutes later, the phone rang again.
They accepted the offer.

That moment confirmed something I'd already begun learning, that intuition doesn't always come through logic or spreadsheets. Sometimes it speaks through dreams, symbols, feelings, or a deep inner knowing that defies explanation. And when we listen, it can save us from making costly mistakes, emotionally, financially, and energetically.

We trusted. We acted. And we saved thirty thousand dollars by following a whisper from within.

**Client Story: Julie - Learning to Listen Again**

As a child, and well into my early twenties, I had a strong connection with my intuition. She was always there, guiding me quietly, giving gentle nudges that helped me make decisions and move through life with a sense of ease. But over time, life got busy. Responsibilities piled up. The noise of the outside world grew louder, and I stopped listening. Or maybe I just stopped noticing.

When I began working with Leonie, one of my biggest intentions was to reconnect with that inner voice. I wanted to feel the clarity I once knew. Leonie helped me understand how to distinguish between my intuition and my logical mind, something I didn't even realise I needed help with. We started with the Traffic Light Game, which at first felt light and fun, but soon became a powerful foundation.

From there, I began tuning into my body, noticing how I was breathing, where I was holding tension, and what happened internally when I was moving too fast. I experimented with journaling, after-work walks (sometimes with music, sometimes in silence), and even slowed down my walking pace in the office to bring a sense of space into my day. During our sessions, we reflected on real moments from my week and unpacked what was truly happening beneath the surface. That's when the awareness really started to land.

One of my first big lessons came at work. I was asked to pass on a message from one of my managers to a colleague, some feedback and a task that involved another team. Somehow, the responsibility bounced back to me. I was told to be the one to deliver the message, even though it wasn't mine.

As soon as I got the direction, I felt that twist in my stomach. A tightening. A clear sense of discomfort. My body was trying to tell me, *"This isn't right."* But I brushed it aside. I told myself I couldn't say no to a manager. So I sent the email, carefully worded, polite, professional.

The response was instant. The message got circulated, reacted to, and escalated all the way to the top. And there I was, caught in the middle of something that had nothing to do with me. My face flushed with embarrassment, but more than anything, I felt the sting of knowing. I *knew* it wouldn't go well. I'd felt it. And I didn't listen.

That experience became a turning point. I started paying attention to that physical signal, that twist in my gut, and I began to honour it.

The lesson deepened a few weeks later when I was headed to the airport for a long-awaited retreat. I'd booked the flight myself, which I've done dozens of times before. But something about this one felt… off. I had hesitated for weeks before booking. I kept looking up the flights but never clicking "purchase." Then, during a rushed lunch break, I booked them quickly on my phone. I remember feeling uneasy as I clicked confirm. I double-checked the *day*, Monday the 17$^{th}$, but not the month.

As it turned out, February and March had the same dates that year. I had booked the flight for the wrong month.

At the airport, things kept going wrong. My Uber cancelled. I was late (which never happens). I couldn't check in online or at the kiosk. By the time I made it to the counter, the agent looked at me with kindness and said, *"Your flight is actually for next month."*

My heart dropped.

As she handed me a phone number for customer support, I felt panic rising, but my awareness stepped in. I reminded myself, *Be kind. Breathe. This isn't her fault. You'll figure it out.*

I couldn't process the rebooking info at the airport, so I went home. I sat on the couch, replayed the moment I booked the ticket, and there it was again, that same feeling in my body. That quiet nudge I had ignored.

And I smiled. I said out loud, *"I hear you now. Lesson learned."*

I sorted the flights, missed the holiday park, but made it to the retreat, and with it, a deeper sense of self-trust.

Now, when I feel that signal in my body, the subtle unease, the quiet nudge, I don't dismiss it. I listen. And more often than not, it's exactly what I need to hear.

## CHAPTER 12

## THE A.I. CODE IN THE GROWTH INDUSTRY

> *"The greatest shift we can offer our clients isn't more information, it's the power to see clearly and feel guided from within. Awareness and intuition aren't extras; they're the foundation. Teach that first, and everything else transforms."*
>
> *-Leonie Du Toit*

**Reimagining the Path to Inner Connection**

For decades, the personal growth industry has helped people reconnect with themselves, through coaching, healing, therapy, and countless spiritual practices. Many of us who are now leaders and facilitators walked our own long, winding journeys toward awareness and being connected to our intuition. We meditated, journaled, healed, studied, and sat in our shadows until the light cracked through. It took years. Sometimes decades.

And in many ways, that path gave us wisdom and depth. But something new is emerging.

What if we could collapse time for our clients, not by skipping the work, but by giving them a heads-up, a cheat sheet, if you will? What if, instead of spending the first months of any program helping someone feel "ready," we guided them straight into a connection with their own inner guidance system?

What would shift if awareness and intuition weren't scattered mentions throughout a program, but the actual starting point?

This is the premise of the A.I. Code.

When we teach clients how to build awareness of their thoughts, behaviours, and energy, and pair that with intuitive guidance they can access daily, they no longer need to rely on us for answers. They become their own source of clarity. And that's when real transformation can happen.

Think about it.

With awareness, we don't take six weeks, like we did in the beginning of our journey, to process the anger over something a friend said from their place of trauma. When it happens, we see it clearly for what it is in the moment, and we can release it instantly. No long, drawn-out days, sleepless nights and churning thoughts.

So why can't we offer this to our clients?

Why can't we give them the code, the actual process, for instant transformation?

Too often, personal development focuses on mindset hacks, belief rewiring, goal setting, and strategy. But without awareness, these tools are surface-level, and without intuition, they're unsustainable.

To make it clear, let's imagine this:

Right now, most coaches are handing their clients a beautiful stack of bricks, roof frames, tiles, cupboards, each one representing a new tool, belief, or habit. These are all amazing pieces for building their new life, but their clients are standing on unstable ground. Some are in a forest, with roots and branches in the way. Others are on soft beach sand or on rocky, uneven mountain terrain. They start laying their bricks, hoping to build a solid wall, but the wall wobbles. It leans. It needs constant support from more sticks and poles to hold everything together.

The foundation was never cleared. The ground was never levelled.

But if, instead, we taught them how to clear the space first, to become aware of their internal landscape and tune into what's really going on, we'd be giving them the tools to create solid ground. Awareness helps us see the landscape, and intuition helps us clear and level the ground to build a sturdy house.

Together, awareness and intuition allow the bricks to stack with strength and alignment.

This is what the A.I. Code does. It doesn't replace what you teach, it strengthens it. It grounds it. It helps your clients actually integrate it.

Imagine a world where every coach, mentor, and teacher started here, with awareness and intuition as the baseline. Not the end goal. What kind of ripple effect would that create?

**What's Missing and Why It Matters**

For an industry so focused on transformation, it's surprising how often awareness and intuition are mentioned as afterthoughts, if at all.

I've studied the most popular teachings in the manifesting space. I've broken down the step-by-step formulas from the industry's top names, people with massive audiences, big promises, and shiny testimonials. And not once did I see them talk about true awareness or inner guidance as the starting point.

They speak about getting clear, raising your vibration, visualising your goals, and taking aligned action. But how do you get clear? What are you aligning with if you're not connected to your inner truth?

It's like telling someone to drive across the country without giving them a map, or even asking where they want to go. You might get somewhere, but is it where your soul was calling you?

Over the years, I've worked with thousands of clients who had done the courses, read the books, journaled their vision boards into existence, and yet still felt lost. Still felt stuck. Still didn't trust themselves.

And I could see exactly why. They had been taught *what* to do, but not how to hear their own soul. They were building tools on top of emotional clutter, energetic noise, and nervous system disconnection.

Awareness is what lets you see where you are. Intuition is what guides you forward. Without those, even the best program can only go so far.

And this doesn't just apply to manifesting. We see it in business coaching, spiritual healing, leadership mentoring, even trauma work. Awareness and intuition are often mentioned in passing, but rarely taught.

I once had a client in a high-level business mastermind come to me privately and say, "I've done everything they told me to do. But I don't feel like *me* in any of it." When we unpacked it, she realised she had been building a business from someone else's blueprint, following someone else's idea of success. No wonder it didn't feel right.

The moment she connected with her own inner knowing, when she stopped outsourcing her answers and started tuning in, everything shifted. Her offers changed. Her messaging changed. And most importantly, her energy changed. She started attracting clients who felt like soul matches because she was finally showing up in alignment with herself.

This is the power of the A.I. Code.

Imagine what could happen if more leaders built it into their teachings. What if, instead of saving awareness and intuition for the occasional meditation or mindset bonus, we embedded it into the foundation of our client work?

We wouldn't just help people get results. We'd help them come home to themselves.

**A Call for Change**

I believe the growth industry is on the edge of its next evolution.

For too long, we've measured success by how many steps someone follows, how many journal prompts they complete, or how well they can reframe their thoughts. But real transformation isn't about ticking boxes, it's about returning to the truth of who you are.

And that's exactly what awareness and intuition give us.

When I look around at the coaching and spiritual spaces, I see so much potential. So many good-hearted, brilliant leaders creating programs, writing books, leading communities. But I also see an opportunity that keeps getting missed, the opportunity to create lasting transformation by helping our clients build their *inner technology* first.

That's what the A.I. Code is. It's the human blueprint for navigating life, not by rules, but by resonance.

Here's what I know to be true:

You can give your clients all the best tools in the world, but if they're not aware of the beliefs driving their choices, or they don't trust the guidance whispering from within, those tools won't land. They won't integrate. They won't stick.

We've built an industry that's often focused on doing, on implementation, on external markers of success, on transformation as an outcome. But what if we started focusing more on *being*, on the quality of someone's relationship with themselves?

When we teach awareness and intuition as core life skills, not as spiritual fluff or extras, we're equipping our clients to live in alignment, not just act in alignment. We're not just helping them get the job, launch the program, or find the relationship. We're helping them *know* if it's right for them. We're helping them move with confidence, even when the path isn't clear.

This is how we create sustainable change.

This is how we evolve the growth industry from information-heavy to transformation-deep.

It's not about replacing what already works. It's about upgrading it to achieve even better outcomes.

My invitation to every coach, teacher, healer, and leader reading this is simple: bring the A.I. Code into your work—not as a footnote but as a foundation.

When we teach people to access their own awareness and intuition first, before the affirmations, the funnels, the steps, the plans, we change lives from the inside out.

And that's how our work creates a bigger impact in this world.

**Bringing the A.I. Code into Practice**

This isn't just a call for awareness. It's a call for integration.

We can't just *talk* about awareness and intuition in passing anymore; we need to teach it, model it, and build it into the very structure of our programs and practices.

And that's exactly why I created **The A.I. Code Integration Guide**, a ready-to-use framework designed to help you bring Awareness and Intuition back into your programs, courses, and client experiences.

Inside the guide, you'll find:

- The foundational tools I use to teach awareness and intuition
- Easy-to-implement exercises like the Traffic Light Game and First Thought Redirect
- Journal structures, reflection prompts, and integration questions
- A clear framework to help your clients shift from unconscious patterns to conscious creation

This isn't about adding more content. It's about making your current content land deeper, because when your clients can see and sense for themselves, they stop relying on you and start leading themselves.

That's the future of this work.
And it starts with us, the ones who've already seen what's possible.

You can grab the A.I. Code Integration Guide from my website — www.leoniedutoit.com — and start weaving these tools into your client experiences today.

And if you're an individual reading this, not a coach, not a healer, not a leader, this guide can still change your life. Use it for yourself. Share it with your family. Start there.

Let's build this new foundation together.

Let's revolutionise growth and healing, from the inside out.

## CHAPTER 13

## THE REVOLUTION

> *"The real uprising isn't external. It's a human being who chooses to walk in awareness and trust their soul."*
>
> -Leonie Du Toit

We are standing at the edge of a new era, not just a shift in technology or culture, but a deep soul-level awakening. This is the Awareness and Intuition Revolution.

For too long, the world has been shaped by systems that reward noise over knowing, speed over stillness, and logic over truth. We've been taught to outsource our answers, follow external formulas, and silence our inner voice in favour of what's proven, profitable, or popular. But this revolution is changing that, not through protest or pressure, but through presence.

It begins in the moments when you choose to pause instead of reacting, to notice instead of being numb, to feel instead of forcing. It starts the first time you question your first thought of the day or when you decide to play the Traffic Light Game in order to build your connection to your inner voice, when you follow a nudge that defies logic but aligns with your soul.

The Spiritual A.I. Revolution is not about rejecting the modern world. It's about reclaiming the ancient intelligence that lives within you, your Awareness and your Intuition. These aren't soft skills. They are survival skills. Thriving skills. Leading skills. And they are needed now more than ever.

All the reasons *why* this matters come down to one simple truth: **this is how we change the world.**

I don't consider myself deeply connected to the politics of the world. I don't pretend to know how to fix governments or prevent wars. But I do know this: when people reconnect with their own inner strength and truth, when they become aware of how they walk in the world and the ripple effect of their actions, everything changes.

Awareness shifts behaviour. Intuition reshapes decisions. Together, they create a new kind of leadership, one that starts within.

The more people who live this way, the more light we bring to the planet. Not by force, but by frequency. Not by taking sides, but by standing firmly in truth. Not by overpowering others, but by becoming deeply anchored in our own integrity.

This revolution is already underway. Every time someone chooses presence over programming, every time a coach invites their client to turn inward instead of just pushing harder, every time a parent teaches their child to trust their inner voice, we amplify it.

You don't have to be loud to lead it. You just have to live it.

Let your life be the message.
Let your awareness be the invitation.
Let your intuition be the revolution.

## CHAPTER 14

## THE SPIRITUAL A.I. TOOLKIT

Throughout this book, we've explored powerful ideas, stories, and shifts in perception. But true transformation doesn't come from what you *know*; it comes from what you *practice*. Awareness and intuition are not just concepts. They are living, breathing abilities that grow stronger the more you use them.

This chapter is your **Spiritual AI Toolkit**, a collection of every exercise, reflection, and embodied practice shared throughout the book, gathered in one place for easy access. You don't need to do them all at once. Think of this as your soul's resource library. A space you can return to again and again, whether you're feeling disconnected, uncertain, curious, or ready for your next level of growth.

Some of these tools are simple. Others might feel surprisingly deep. But every single one was chosen for one reason: **they work**. They build awareness. They deepen intuition. And they bring you home to yourself.

You've already begun the journey. This is how you keep walking it, one conscious, intuitive step at a time. So put a sticky note in this chapter and keep this book close by in order to access these simple yet powerful ways to help you connect deeper to the power you hold within.

## Chapter 2 Exercises - Awareness: The Key to Everything

### 1. The Inner "Hello" Practice

**Purpose:** To experience yourself as the *observer* and recognise that you are not your thoughts.

**How to Practice:**

- Close your eyes and say "hello" in your mind.
- Now say it louder in your mind.
- Then, shout it mentally like you would from a mountaintop.
- Ask yourself: *Who heard that?*

**Awareness Prompt:**

"If I can observe the thought, then I am not the thought. I am the one noticing."

## 2. Flashlight Awareness Exercise (Awareness vs. Consciousness)

**Purpose:** To understand how awareness and consciousness work together.

**How to Practice:**

- Imagine a dark room, and your awareness is the flashlight.
- Now point that beam toward an object (a memory, a feeling, a thought).
- Notice how your attention brings it into consciousness.

**Awareness Prompt:**

"Where I shine my awareness, my consciousness grows."


## 3. Real-Time Mind Pattern Interrupt

**Purpose:** To disrupt looping thoughts and habitual self-talk with awareness.

**How to Practice:**

- When you notice a reactive or critical thought (e.g., "I'm not good enough"), pause.
- Ask: *Is this thought true? Is it mine? Where did it come from?*
- Breathe, and redirect your attention to your body or breath.

**Awareness Prompt:**

"Awareness creates the space I need to respond instead of react."

## 4. Mirror Moment Awareness

**Purpose:** To shift inner dialogue from criticism to compassion.

**How to Practice:**

- Stand in front of a mirror.
- Notice your first thought.
- If it's critical, pause. Ask yourself: *Is this how I want to speak to myself?*
- Place your hand on your heart and say one kind, true thing.

**Awareness Prompt:**

"This is not the truth. This is not love. This is not me."

## 5. Resistance Check-In

**Purpose:** To gently explore emotional resistance to awareness or truth.

**How to Practice:**

- When you notice avoidance or emotional discomfort, pause and ask:

- What am I resisting right now?
- What truth feels too hard to see?
- Am I afraid something will have to change if I face this?

**Awareness Prompt:**

"Resistance isn't always fear. Sometimes it's wisdom asking me to listen deeper."

## 6. Soul-Based Depression Reflection

**Purpose:** To recognise if depression may be linked to misalignment rather than just mental or chemical factors.

**How to Practice:**

- Journal your honest responses to the following:
- Where in my life do I feel flat, numb, or disconnected?
- Is there something I've been ignoring that I know is out of alignment?
- What does my soul want me to see right now?

**Awareness Prompt:**

"What if my sadness isn't brokenness, but a message asking me to come home to myself?"

## Chapter 3: The How-To of Building Awareness

### 1. First Thought of the Day Practice

*Purpose:* Interrupt autopilot and consciously set the tone for your day.

**Practice:**

As soon as you wake up, pause and observe your first thought. If it's negative or limiting, gently shift it into something intentional.

Example: Shift "I can't do this" to "I'm open to being supported today."

**Tip:** Keep a journal by your bed and write your first thought each morning for 7 days.

### 2. Common Trigger Awareness Journal

*Purpose:* Identify the specific moments, patterns, and situations that regularly pull you out of presence.

**Practice:**

At the end of the day, reflect and write:

- When did I feel pulled out of awareness today?
- What triggered me?
- What did I notice in my body, mind, or energy?

- What would I like to do differently next time?

### 3. Nervous System Regulation Practices
*Purpose:* Reconnect with your body and calm your system in real-time.
**Practices Include:**

- Shake out your hands, arms, or whole body
- Take deep sighing breaths (inhale through the nose, exhale through the mouth with sound)
- Place your hand on your heart or belly and breathe into that space
- Hum, sing, or chant gently
- Walk barefoot or ground your feet into the earth
- Rock or sway slowly to self-soothe

**Use when:** You feel overwhelmed, anxious, frozen, reactive, or scattered.

### 4. Embodiment Check-In
*Purpose:* Build awareness of your personal signs of dysregulation.
**Practice:**
Throughout your day or during reflection time, ask:

- What physical sensations do I notice when I'm triggered or overwhelmed?
- Where in my body do I feel stress or tension first?

- What's one thing I can do to ground myself when I feel this way?

## 5. Awareness Anchors

*Purpose:* Bring yourself back to presence in everyday life.

**Anchors Include:**

- The Pause: One intentional breath before reacting or deciding
- The Breath Drop: Deep breath into the belly to reconnect to the body
- Body Check-In: Notice posture, breath, physical tension, and return to sensation
- Name 3 Things: Name three things you see, hear, and feel right now
- "Is This Mine?": Ask this question when you feel heavy, unclear, or off-centre
- Conscious Transitions: Pause and reset your energy between tasks or environments
- Environmental Cues: Place reminders (sticky notes, crystals, lock screen words) to bring you back
- "Right Now" Mantra: Say silently, "Right now, I am…" and complete the sentence with something true

## 6. The AWARE Method

*A five-step framework to return to conscious presence*

**A - Acknowledge** what you're experiencing without judgment

**W - Witness** it from the perspective of the observer

**A - Ask** what it's pointing to underneath the surface

**R - Regulate** your nervous system and reconnect with your body

**E -Empower** your next choice from a grounded state

**Use it during:** Trigger moments, emotional spirals, or daily reflection to process what's coming up for you.

## Chapter 4 Exercises: Intuition - The Voice of the Soul

### 1. The First-Thought Practice

**Purpose:** To help you distinguish intuition from mental noise by catching intuitive guidance in the first few seconds it arrives.

**How to Practice:**

- Choose a simple decision (e.g., what to wear, what route to take, who to call).
- Ask yourself a clear question.

- Pay close attention to the very first thought, feeling, or nudge that comes, within one to two seconds.
- Notice what comes *after* that initial moment. Is it logic, doubt, or justification?
- Begin journaling the difference between what comes first and what follows. Reflect later on which choice felt most aligned.

## 2. The Intuition Journal

**Purpose:** To track your intuitive hits, how you responded, and what the outcome was, helping to build trust over time.

**How to Use:**

- At the end of each day (or week), write down any intuitive nudges you received.
- Note whether you followed them or not, and what the result was.
- Reflect on how the intuition felt in your body. Was it clear, expansive, quiet?
- This helps you begin recognising your intuitive "voice" more consistently.

## 3. Body Compass Check-In

**Purpose:** To connect with your body as an intuitive instrument and learn how it signals yes or no.

**How to Practice:**

- Sit quietly. Take a few deep breaths.
- Think of a time when you felt deeply aligned or safe. Notice how your body feels when it's a "yes."
- Now, recall a time when something was off or wrong. Notice your body's "no" response.
- Practice checking in with your body on simple decisions and track how it responds.
- Over time, you'll start to recognise the energetic difference between intuitive guidance and nervous system reactions.

**4. The Intuition vs Fear Inquiry**

**Purpose:** To help you tell the difference between intuitive guidance and fear-based reactivity.

**Prompt:**
When you receive guidance or a nudge, ask:

- Is this message calm or emotional?
- Does it feel like expansion or contraction?
- Am I acting from trust or trying to avoid discomfort?
- Is there clarity or confusion behind the feeling?

Use this as a journaling tool or a mental check-in during real-life moments.

### 5. The Awareness + Intuition Reflection

**Purpose:** To understand how these two spirit senses work together and deepen your ability to stay present as guidance unfolds.

**How to Practice:**

- Recall a recent moment when you followed a nudge that made no logical sense, but felt right.
- Reflect: Were you in awareness? Did you stay present after the first hit, or did you lose the thread?
- Ask: If I had remained more aware, would I have noticed the next step sooner?
- Journal what that moment taught you about the dance between intuition and awareness.

## Chapter 5: Strengthening Intuition - The Practice of Listening

### Tools to Build and Strengthen Intuition

### 1. The 4-Step Intuition Cycle

A foundational process for recognising and responding to intuitive guidance.

**Steps:**

- *Receive It* – Be aware and open to intuitive nudges.
- *Acknowledge It* – Name the hit to signal safety and readiness.
- *Act On It* – Take small, aligned action to build trust.
- *Celebrate the Outcome* – Anchor in success and create positive reinforcement.

## 2. The Traffic Light Game

A fast, playful way to walk through all four intuition steps with immediate feedback.

**How to Play:**

- Expect a number to drop into your awareness at a red light.
- Count backwards from that number.
- Notice if the light turns green at 0 or 1.
- Celebrate if it matches. Try again if it doesn't.

**Why It Works:** Builds trust, trains receptivity, and creates a safe space for intuitive practice.

## 3. The One-Second Rule

A daily awareness habit to catch intuitive insight before your logic overrides it.

**How to Use:** Ask small questions throughout your day. Act on the very first impression or answer that arises, without overthinking.

### 4. Intuitive Yes/No Body Scan

A somatic method for reading intuitive signals through physical sensations.

**How to Use:**

- Anchor what a clear "yes" and "no" feel like in your body.
- Ask intuitive questions and feel for expansion or contraction.
- Use with everyday decisions to deepen trust in your internal compass.

### 5. The Random Object Game

A low-pressure, high-fun way to tune in to unseen information.

**How to Play:**

- Have someone place an object in a bag or box.
- Tune in and describe what comes to mind: shape, colour, texture, energy.
- Reveal the object and notice what came through. Focus on receiving, not accuracy.

### 6. The Everyday Nudges Log

A journaling tool to build awareness of how often intuition speaks.

**How to Use:**

- Keep a running list of intuitive nudges throughout your day.
- Note the timing and any validations or outcomes.
- Review weekly to recognise patterns and deepen your confidence.

## 7. The Mirror Drop-In

A soul-connection practice for hearing quiet, honest guidance.
**How to Use:**

- Stand or sit in front of a mirror.
- Soften your gaze and ask, "What do I need to know today?"
- Wait for a response, image, word, feeling, or phrase, and receive it with openness.

## 8. The CLEAR Method

A simple, structured process to strengthen intuitive decision-making in daily life.

**C – Calm** – Breathe and regulate your nervous system.
**L – Listen** – Tune in to the subtle cues in your body.
**E – Enquire** – Ask your higher self or intuition a clear, open question.
**A – Act** – Follow the guidance with aligned action, even if small.
**R – Reflect** – Notice how it felt and what happened as a result.

# Chapter 6: Awareness in Self and Spiritual Development

## Spiritual AI Toolkit – Practices and Exercises

### 1. Rewired Journaling

**Purpose:** Transform journaling from a surface-level release into an intuitive dialogue.

**How to Practice:**

- Before writing, pause and ask: *"What am I not seeing?"* or *"What part of me needs to speak right now?"*
- Use awareness to observe the thoughts and stories coming through without judgment.
- After journaling, sit with the words and ask: *"Is this mine? Is this true?"*
- Listen for subtle intuitive nudges or insights.

### 2. Intuitive Meditation

**Purpose:** Shift meditation from mental control to soul-level listening.

**How to Practice:**

- Sit comfortably and begin with a few minutes of conscious breathing.
- As thoughts arise, practice observing them without attachment - this is awareness in action.
- Set the intention: *"I'm here to listen."*
- Notice if any feelings, images, or inner knowings arise. Gently follow their thread.
- End with: *"What truth did I hear today?"* and write down what came.

## 3. A.I.-Aligned Vision Board Creation

**Purpose:** Build a vision board that reflects your *soul's truth*, not society's expectations.

**How to Practice:**

- Before starting, close your eyes and ask your intuition: *"What actually excites me?"*
- Tune into how your body feels when you see different images or words, and awareness will show you what resonates.
- Only include what feels like a full-body *yes*.
- Once your board is complete, spend a few moments daily connecting with how it *feels*, not just how it looks.

## 4. Compassionate Shadow Work Check-In

**Purpose:** Engage with your shadow through the lens of awareness and intuition.

**How to Practice:**

- When you feel emotionally activated, write or reflect on:
- *What does this remind me of?*
- *What part of me is hurting?*
- *What belief or fear is being poked here?*

- Pause and breathe into the discomfort with compassion.
- Ask your intuition: *"What is this here to teach me?"* or *"What truth is underneath this reaction?"*

## 5. Embodied Nervous System Awareness

**Purpose:** Choose nervous system tools that are right for you, in the moment.

**How to Practice:**

- When triggered or dysregulated, pause and check in:
- *What is my body asking for right now?*
- *Do I need stillness, movement, breath, or sound?*
- Use awareness to notice how your body responds to different practices.
- Let your intuition guide you to what feels most

supportive, not just what worked last time.

## 6. Truth-Aligned Affirmation Audit

**Purpose:** Use awareness to make affirmations feel real, not forced.

**How to Practice:**

- Say your affirmation aloud (e.g. *"I am abundant."*)
- Notice your body's response. Does it relax or tighten?
- If there's resistance, ask: *"What would feel more honest right now?"*
- Adjust the affirmation to one that still moves you forward but feels true, e.g.
  - *"I am learning to receive abundance."*
  - *"I am becoming more open to support."*

## 7. Timeline of My Life (Life Purpose Reflection Exercise)

**Purpose:** Use awareness to discover patterns, gifts, and clues to your soul's purpose.

**How to Practice:**

- Take several sheets of paper and tape them together, or use a large whiteboard.
- Create a timeline from birth to now. Add key life events, memories, and milestones — both joyful and painful.

- Reflect on:
- What themes or patterns keep showing up?
- What challenges shaped my strengths?
- Where have I always felt called, even quietly?
- Ask your intuition: *"What thread connects all of this?"*

## 8. Soul Purpose Reflection Questions

**Purpose:** Clarify the deeper calling that may already be expressing itself through your life.

**Questions to Reflect or Journal On:**

- What do people often thank me for?
- What kind of advice do others naturally seek from me?
- What do people consistently come to me for?
- Are there issues in the world that deeply frustrate or move me?
- What personal challenges have I already overcome?
- What transformation have I been through that I could now guide others through?

# Chapter 7 Exercises: Awareness in Healing - The Body-Mind Connection and Health

## 1. Daily Body Awareness Check-In

**Purpose:** Strengthen awareness of physical sensations and begin dialoguing with the body.

**How to Practice:**

- Close your eyes and take a slow breath.
- Ask: *What's happening in my body right now?*
- Gently scan from head to toe, noticing areas of tightness, discomfort, or stillness.
- Place your hand on any area that stands out and ask: *What might you be trying to say?*
- No need to fix, just notice and listen.

## 2. Awareness Through Language

**Purpose:** Reframe the way you talk about illness, pain, and healing.

**Practice Prompts:**

- Notice every time you say, *"I have..."* or *"I am..."* in relation to a diagnosis or symptom.
- Pause and ask: *Is this an experience I'm going through, or an identity I've claimed?*
- Replace phrases like *"I'm sick"* with *"I'm recovering from..."* or *"My body is healing..."*

### 3. Translating the Body's Language

**Purpose:** Use common expressions to gain insight into what your body may be trying to communicate.

**How to Practice:**

- Reflect on phrases you use like *"pain in the neck," "sick to my stomach,"* or *"heavy shoulders."*
- Ask yourself:
- *Where do I feel this in my body right now?*
- *Is there an emotion or situation that connects to it?*
- Use the provided list of 20 common body idioms (see Chapter 7) as a reference tool.

### 4. Track Your Body's Signals

**Purpose:** Build intuitive pattern recognition between emotional, mental, and physical states.

**How to Practice:**

- Keep a daily note or journal of:
- Physical sensations or symptoms
- Emotional state
- Recent foods, decisions, or stressful moments
- Review weekly to notice patterns and insights.

## 5. Translation Prompt

**Purpose:** Strengthen intuitive insight into symptoms.

**When a symptom arises, ask:**

- *If this part of my body could speak, what would it say?*
- *What emotion or memory might be living here?*
- *What's the most loving way I can respond right now?*

## 6. Chapter Reflection Questions

**Use these for deeper integration or journaling:**

- What is one area of my body I've been ignoring or avoiding?
- What might that part of me need: attention, rest, expression, love?
- If I trusted that my body was on my side, how would I treat it differently?

# Chapter 8 – Awareness in Relationships and Partnerships

**Practices & Tools**

## 1. Spot the Pattern

A reflection exercise to help you identify unconscious relationship habits.

**Prompts:**

- What are some things I expect from my partner that I haven't clearly communicated?
- Do I ever feel resentful for not getting something… that I've never actually asked for?
- When I feel triggered in a relationship, what's my first instinct: to blame, withdraw, control, or prove?
- Have I been trying to earn love by being perfect, giving too much, or abandoning my own needs?
- Where have I handed over responsibility for my happiness?

Ask yourself: *"What would this look like if I showed up with awareness instead?"*


## 2. The Sacred Pause

A practice for interrupting reactive moments with presence and emotional responsibility.

**Steps:**

1. Notice the emotional charge rising in your body.

2. Pause and say:

*"Something's coming up inside me, and I just need a moment. I'm becoming aware of something in me that wants to react, and I want to understand what it is before I respond."*

3. Breathe. Tune into your body. Ask:

- What am I feeling right now?
- Is this about the present moment, or something from the past?
- What do I actually need right now?

4. Return to the conversation from clarity, not emotion.

### 3. Am I Projecting or Communicating?

A quick internal checklist before you speak in emotionally charged moments.

**You're likely projecting if:**

- You speak from emotional charge without reflection.
- You use blame, exaggeration, or absolute language (e.g. "you never…").
- You want to be right more than you want to be understood.

**You're likely communicating if:**

- You pause before speaking.
- You take ownership of your feelings with "I" language.
- You're expressing truth and inviting connection, not trying to control.

## 4. How Do I Give and Receive Love?

An awareness practice for understanding and aligning love languages.

**Reflective Prompts:**

- How do I naturally show love in relationships?
- How do I feel most loved and seen?
- Have I expected my partner to love me the way I love them?
- Am I paying attention to how *they* receive love?
- What might shift if I became more present to their needs?

## 5. What Am I Practising in This Relationship?

A moment-to-moment awareness tool to bring clarity to your patterns.

**Ask Yourself:**

- What am I practising right now, curiosity or control? Patience or defensiveness?
- Is this how I want to keep showing up?
- What would a more conscious version of me choose instead?

## 6. Bringing Awareness to Your Habits

A journaling exercise to uncover the roots of emotional habits in your relationship.

**Prompts:**

- What habits have I carried into this relationship that no longer serve me?
- Where did I learn these patterns?
- Are they rooted in love or in fear?
- What healthier, more aware responses am I ready to practice?

## 7. Close the Gaps

A reflection tool to identify where disconnection is forming.

**Ask Yourself:**

- Have I stopped showing up in meaningful ways?
- Are there things I've been too tired, too scared, or too distracted to say?
- Is there a growing space between us that I've been pretending not to see?
- What small act of love or presence could I offer today to help close that gap?

## 8. Practice: Bringing Awareness into Your Relationship

A complete, step-by-step practice for everyday conscious relating.

**Steps:**

**1. Pause before reacting.**

*What am I feeling, and where is it in my body?*

**2. Check in with your thoughts.**

*What story am I telling myself about this?*

**3. Speak with clarity and care.**

*Use "I" language to share, not accuse.*

**4. Ask for feedback.**

*"What did you hear when I said that?"*

**5. Reflect afterwards.**

*What was I really practising in that moment? And is it aligned with who I want to be in love?*

# Chapter 9 – Awareness With and In Our Children

## 1. The Morning Thought Redirect (Parent + Child Practice)

Invite your child to become aware of the first thought they have when they wake up. Together, gently notice it, and if it's unhelpful or negative, practise choosing a more empowering thought.

**Purpose:** Builds self-awareness and the ability to shift energy intentionally at the start of the day.

**2. The Traffic Light Game (Parent + Child Practice)**

Play the traffic light game in the car with then kids. They will love it!

**Purpose:** Strengthens intuitive listening in a playful, low-pressure way.

**3. The Parking Game (Family Intuition Practice)**

When driving to a destination, ask your child to tune in and feel where you'll find a parking spot — which side, how far down, or how close to the entrance.

**Purpose:** Builds intuitive confidence and helps children experience accurate inner knowing.

**4. "Is This Mine?" Energy Check-In**

When your child feels unwell or emotionally off, ask them to pause and check in with the question: *"Is this mine?"* This helps them discern if they're picking up someone else's energy or emotion.

**Purpose:** Teaches energetic boundaries and the ability to release what doesn't belong to them.

### 5. Emotional Awareness Reflection (Conversation Prompt)

Use simple, curious questions to explore what your child is feeling and why. For example, "When that happened, how did you feel in your body?" or "What do you think your feeling is trying to tell you?"

**Purpose:** Encourages emotional awareness and creates space for inner guidance to be recognised.

## Chapter 10 – Awakening Abundance

### 1. Aligned Clarity Practice

Get crystal clear on what you want and why. Write down one desire in full detail, including sensory details, emotional resonance, and the reasons it matters to you. Then ask: *What feeling am I really chasing underneath this?* Name it.

## 2. The Car Exercise (Specific Manifesting)

Choose something tangible you want to manifest, like a car. Write down every detail: make, model, year, colour, features, etc. Then go test drive it or interact with it physically if possible. Visualize daily as if it's already yours, see yourself using it in everyday life.

## 3. The Gratitude Activation

Each morning, before starting your day, list three things you're grateful for *as if they've already arrived.* This anchors your frequency to receiving. (e.g., "I'm so grateful for the freedom my business gives me.")

## 4. The "Trust Leap" Reflection

Reflect on a current decision where your logic and your intuition are pulling in different directions. Journal:

- *What does my soul want here?*
- *What am I afraid will happen if I trust it?*
- *Where is the feeling of expansion?*

This will help you practice choosing alignment over fear.

## 5. The Surrender Letter

Write a letter to God/The Universe that starts with: *"Here's what I desire, and here's what I'm letting go of..."*
Name what you're giving over (the timeline, the how, the fear),

and end with: *"I trust you to handle the rest."*

### 6. From Stuck to Shifted: Getting Unstuck Checklist
When you're feeling low or blocked, choose one or more of the following:
- Move your body (walk, dance, shake it out)
- Change your environment (go outside, open windows)
- Breathe consciously (try box breathing or deep exhale)
- Do something small but empowering (make your bed, reply to that message, light a candle)
- Help someone else (shift your energy from lack to generosity)
- Ground yourself with the 3-minute awareness scan

### 7. Awareness Scan for Competing Desires
Ask yourself:

- *Do I have any conflicting beliefs about this desire?*
- *Am I trying to manifest two opposing things?*

Journal through any mixed messages you might be sending, and choose to realign.

BONUS

CHAPTER 15

**STEPPING INTO AWARENESS AND INTUITION**

Awareness and intuition are not just ideas to understand; they are practices to embody. The more you use them, the stronger they become. That's why I created this 30-Day Diary, to give you a space to *live* what you've just read, to integrate these spirit senses into your everyday life in a simple, yet powerful way.

This journal is not about getting it "right." It's about showing up, gently, consistently, and with curiosity.

Each day invites you to notice your first thought in the morning (an anchor point for awareness), reflect on what showed up throughout your day, and record any intuitive nudges or hits you received. There's also space to ground your energy with gratitude — one of the most potent ways to stay connected to the present moment.

Use this as a tool for deepening your connection to yourself. Let it become a mirror, a compass, and a quiet guide as you continue awakening your inner intelligence.

And here's the best part: you can return to this diary again and again. Every new season of your life will bring different layers of insight. The more you use it, the more attuned you'll become. Over time, you'll begin to notice patterns, strengthen your inner trust, and build a deeper relationship with your soul's voice.

So, take these next 30 days slowly, intentionally. You don't need to force anything. Just be present with what comes.

This is where the real transformation begins.

## 30 DAY AWARENESS AND INTUITION DIARY

### Day 1

Morning:

*"Awareness is the first step to healing."*

What were your first thoughts when you opened your eyes? How does your body feel this morning? What emotions are present as you start your day? What are you most grateful for as you begin this day?

------------------------------------------------------------
------------------------------------------------------------
------------------------------------------------------------
------------------------------------------------------------
------------------------------------------------------------
------------------------------------------------------------

Evening:

*"Intuition is seeing with the soul."* – Dean Koontz

Reflect on a moment today when you had a subtle knowing. What did it feel like

------------------------------------------------------------
------------------------------------------------------------
------------------------------------------------------------
------------------------------------------------------------
------------------------------------------------------------
------------------------------------------------------------

## Day 2

Morning:

*"The more aware you are, the more control you have over your life." – Deepak Chopra*

What were your first thoughts when you opened your eyes? How does your body feel this morning? What emotions are present as you start your day? What are you most grateful for as you begin this day?

------------------------------------------------------------
------------------------------------------------------------
------------------------------------------------------------
------------------------------------------------------------
------------------------------------------------------------
------------------------------------------------------------

Evening:

*"Your intuition knows what to write, so get out of the way." – Ray Bradbury*

Did you notice any recurring thoughts or emotions today? Did you act on an intuitive nudge today? What was the outcome?

------------------------------------------------------------
------------------------------------------------------------
------------------------------------------------------------
------------------------------------------------------------
------------------------------------------------------------
------------------------------------------------------------

**Day 3**

Morning:

*"Your body speaks to you; awareness is the key to understanding its language."*

What were your first thoughts when you opened your eyes? How does your body feel this morning? What emotions are present as you start your day? What are you most grateful for as you begin this day?

------------------------------------------------------------------------
------------------------------------------------------------------------
------------------------------------------------------------------------
------------------------------------------------------------------------
------------------------------------------------------------------------
------------------------------------------------------------------------

Evening:

*"The body never lies." – Martha Graham*

How did your body guide you today? Where did you feel your inner yes or no?

------------------------------------------------------------------------
------------------------------------------------------------------------
------------------------------------------------------------------------
------------------------------------------------------------------------
------------------------------------------------------------------------
------------------------------------------------------------------------
------------------------------------------------------------------------

**Day 4**

Morning:

*"Awareness is like the sun. When it shines on things, they are transformed." – Thich Nhat Hanh*

What were your first thoughts when you opened your eyes? How does your body feel this morning? What emotions are present as you start your day? What are you most grateful for as you begin this day?

---------------------------------------------------------------
---------------------------------------------------------------
---------------------------------------------------------------
---------------------------------------------------------------
---------------------------------------------------------------
---------------------------------------------------------------

Evening:

*"At times you have to leave the noisy world and get back to your intuition."*

When did you feel a quiet inner voice speak to you? What did it say? What was the most significant moment of awareness you experienced today?

---------------------------------------------------------------
---------------------------------------------------------------
---------------------------------------------------------------
---------------------------------------------------------------
---------------------------------------------------------------
---------------------------------------------------------------

**Day 5**

Morning:

*"In awareness, you find your power."*

What were your first thoughts when you opened your eyes? How does your body feel this morning? What emotions are present as you start your day? What are you most grateful for as you begin this day?

------------------------------------------------------------
------------------------------------------------------------
------------------------------------------------------------
------------------------------------------------------------
------------------------------------------------------------
------------------------------------------------------------

Evening:

*"The intuitive mind is a sacred gift."* – Albert Einstein

How did you respond to challenges today? Were you able to remain aware and present? Did you override your intuition at any point today? What happened?

------------------------------------------------------------
------------------------------------------------------------
------------------------------------------------------------
------------------------------------------------------------
------------------------------------------------------------
------------------------------------------------------------

**Day 6**

Morning:

*"Awareness is the greatest agent for change."* – Eckhart Tolle

What were your first thoughts when you opened your eyes? How does your body feel this morning? What emotions are present as you start your day? What are you most grateful for as you begin this day?

------------------------------------------------------------
------------------------------------------------------------
------------------------------------------------------------
------------------------------------------------------------
------------------------------------------------------------
------------------------------------------------------------

Evening:

*"Your first instinct is usually the right one."*

What did you learn about yourself today? What was your first intuitive thought this morning? Did you follow it?

------------------------------------------------------------
------------------------------------------------------------
------------------------------------------------------------
------------------------------------------------------------
------------------------------------------------------------
------------------------------------------------------------
------------------------------------------------------------
------------------------------------------------------------

**Day 7**

Morning:

*"Presence is a gift you give to yourself and the world."*

What were your first thoughts when you opened your eyes? How does your body feel this morning? What emotions are present as you start your day? What are you most grateful for as you begin this day?

------------------------------------------------------------
------------------------------------------------------------
------------------------------------------------------------
------------------------------------------------------------
------------------------------------------------------------
------------------------------------------------------------

Evening:

*"Doubt kills more dreams than failure ever will."*

How did you experience resistance or doubt around your intuition today? Were there any moments today when you felt fully present?

------------------------------------------------------------
------------------------------------------------------------
------------------------------------------------------------
------------------------------------------------------------
------------------------------------------------------------
------------------------------------------------------------

**Day 8**

Morning:

*"The key to growth is the introduction of higher dimensions of consciousness into our awareness." – Lao Tzu*

What were your first thoughts when you opened your eyes? How does your body feel this morning? What emotions are present as you start your day? What are you most grateful for as you begin this day?

---------------------------------------------------------------
---------------------------------------------------------------
---------------------------------------------------------------
---------------------------------------------------------------
---------------------------------------------------------------
---------------------------------------------------------------

Evening:

*"Trust your hunches. They're usually based on facts filed away just below the conscious level." – Joyce Brothers*

How did your emotions influence your actions today? Was there a moment today where logic and intuition conflicted? Which did you follow?

---------------------------------------------------------------
---------------------------------------------------------------
---------------------------------------------------------------
---------------------------------------------------------------
---------------------------------------------------------------
---------------------------------------------------------------

**Day 9**

Morning:

*"Patterns repeat until awareness breaks the cycle."*

What were your first thoughts when you opened your eyes? How does your body feel this morning? What emotions are present as you start your day? What are you most grateful for as you begin this day?

------------------------------------------------------------------------
------------------------------------------------------------------------
------------------------------------------------------------------------
------------------------------------------------------------------------
------------------------------------------------------------------------
------------------------------------------------------------------------

Evening:

*"Silence is the language of intuition."*

Did you notice any patterns in your thoughts or behaviour today? What external noise tried to drown out your inner voice today?

------------------------------------------------------------------------
------------------------------------------------------------------------
------------------------------------------------------------------------
------------------------------------------------------------------------
------------------------------------------------------------------------
------------------------------------------------------------------------
------------------------------------------------------------------------
------------------------------------------------------------------------

## Day 10

Morning:

*"Peace comes from being in alignment with your true self." – Wayne Dyer*

What were your first thoughts when you opened your eyes? How does your body feel this morning? What emotions are present as you start your day? What are you most grateful for as you begin this day?

---
---
---
---
---
---

Evening:

*"Sometimes, intuition whispers the truth before your mind can argue it away."*

What was the most peaceful moment of your day? What insight came to you that felt like it came from nowhere?

---
---
---
---
---
---

**Day 11**

Morning:

*"Your outer world is a reflection of your inner awareness."*
What were your first thoughts when you opened your eyes? How does your body feel this morning? What emotions are present as you start your day? What are you most grateful for as you begin this day?

------------------------------------------------------------------
------------------------------------------------------------------
------------------------------------------------------------------
------------------------------------------------------------------
------------------------------------------------------------------
------------------------------------------------------------------

Evening:

*"Dreams are illustrations... from the book your soul is writing."* – Marsha Norman
How did your interactions with others reflect your inner state? Did you have a dream last night that felt meaningful? What might it be showing you?

------------------------------------------------------------------
------------------------------------------------------------------
------------------------------------------------------------------
------------------------------------------------------------------
------------------------------------------------------------------
------------------------------------------------------------------

**Day 12**

Morning:

*"Awareness brings clarity, and with clarity comes transformation."*

What were your first thoughts when you opened your eyes? How does your body feel this morning? What emotions are present as you start your day? What are you most grateful for as you begin this day?

------------------------------------------------------------
------------------------------------------------------------
------------------------------------------------------------
------------------------------------------------------------
------------------------------------------------------------
------------------------------------------------------------

Evening:

*"Learning to trust your intuition is an art form."*

What surprised you about your awareness today? What part of you do you find hardest to trust? What is that part trying to protect?

------------------------------------------------------------
------------------------------------------------------------
------------------------------------------------------------
------------------------------------------------------------
------------------------------------------------------------
------------------------------------------------------------
------------------------------------------------------------

**Day 13**

Morning:

*"The present moment is the gateway to awareness."*

What were your first thoughts when you opened your eyes? How does your body feel this morning? What emotions are present as you start your day? What are you most grateful for as you begin this day?

------------------------------------------------------------
------------------------------------------------------------
------------------------------------------------------------
------------------------------------------------------------
------------------------------------------------------------
------------------------------------------------------------

Evening:

*"Intuition doesn't tell you what you want to hear; it tells you what you need to hear."*

How did you ground yourself in the present moment today? What small decision did you make today from a place of instinct or feeling?

------------------------------------------------------------
------------------------------------------------------------
------------------------------------------------------------
------------------------------------------------------------
------------------------------------------------------------
------------------------------------------------------------
------------------------------------------------------------

**Day 14**

Morning:

*Energy flows where awareness goes." – Tony Robbins*

What were your first thoughts when you opened your eyes? How does your body feel this morning? What emotions are present as you start your day? What are you most grateful for as you begin this day?

---------------------------------------------------------------------
---------------------------------------------------------------------
---------------------------------------------------------------------
---------------------------------------------------------------------
---------------------------------------------------------------------
---------------------------------------------------------------------

Evening:

*"The quieter you become, the more you can hear." – Ram Dass*

Where did you sense your intuition physically in your body today? What did you discover about your energy levels and how they shifted today?

---------------------------------------------------------------------
---------------------------------------------------------------------
---------------------------------------------------------------------
---------------------------------------------------------------------
---------------------------------------------------------------------
---------------------------------------------------------------------
---------------------------------------------------------------------

**Day 15**

Morning:

*"With awareness, every decision becomes a conscious choice."*
What were your first thoughts when you opened your eyes? How does your body feel this morning? What emotions are present as you start your day? What are you most grateful for as you begin this day?

------------------------------------------------------------
------------------------------------------------------------
------------------------------------------------------------
------------------------------------------------------------
------------------------------------------------------------
------------------------------------------------------------

Evening:

*"The intuitive mind speaks softly — listen closely."*
What message did you ignore today? How do you know it was your intuition? How did awareness influence your decisions today?

------------------------------------------------------------
------------------------------------------------------------
------------------------------------------------------------
------------------------------------------------------------
------------------------------------------------------------
------------------------------------------------------------
------------------------------------------------------------
------------------------------------------------------------

**Day 16**

Morning:

*"In stillness, awareness is revealed."*

What were your first thoughts when you opened your eyes? How does your body feel this morning? What emotions are present as you start your day? What are you most grateful for as you begin this day?

------------------------------------------------------------------------
------------------------------------------------------------------------
------------------------------------------------------------------------
------------------------------------------------------------------------
------------------------------------------------------------------------
------------------------------------------------------------------------

Evening:

*"You know the truth by the way it feels."*

Did you find moments of stillness in your day? What would your intuition have you do differently today if you had listened to it first?

------------------------------------------------------------------------
------------------------------------------------------------------------
------------------------------------------------------------------------
------------------------------------------------------------------------
------------------------------------------------------------------------
------------------------------------------------------------------------
------------------------------------------------------------------------
------------------------------------------------------------------------

**Day 17**

Morning:

*"Awareness and compassion go hand in hand."*

What were your first thoughts when you opened your eyes? How does your body feel this morning? What emotions are present as you start your day? What are you most grateful for as you begin this day?

---------------------------------------------------------------
---------------------------------------------------------------
---------------------------------------------------------------
---------------------------------------------------------------
---------------------------------------------------------------
---------------------------------------------------------------

Evening:

*"Symbols are the language of the soul."*

How did you show compassion to yourself or others today? What image or symbol stayed with you today? What might it represent?

---------------------------------------------------------------
---------------------------------------------------------------
---------------------------------------------------------------
---------------------------------------------------------------
---------------------------------------------------------------
---------------------------------------------------------------
---------------------------------------------------------------

**Day 18**

Morning:

*"Awareness transforms mistakes into lessons."*

What were your first thoughts when you opened your eyes? How does your body feel this morning? What emotions are present as you start your day? What are you most grateful for as you begin this day?

------------------------------------------------------------------------
------------------------------------------------------------------------
------------------------------------------------------------------------
------------------------------------------------------------------------
------------------------------------------------------------------------
------------------------------------------------------------------------

Evening:

*Clarity comes when you pause to listen within."*

What did you learn from any mistakes or challenges you faced today? Was there a moment of unexpected clarity today? Describe it.

------------------------------------------------------------------------
------------------------------------------------------------------------
------------------------------------------------------------------------
------------------------------------------------------------------------
------------------------------------------------------------------------
------------------------------------------------------------------------
------------------------------------------------------------------------

**Day 19**

Morning:

*"Conscious communication begins with awareness."*

What were your first thoughts when you opened your eyes? How does your body feel this morning? What emotions are present as you start your day? What are you most grateful for as you begin this day?

------------------------------------------------------------------------
------------------------------------------------------------------------
------------------------------------------------------------------------
------------------------------------------------------------------------
------------------------------------------------------------------------
------------------------------------------------------------------------

Evening:

*"First impressions are the whispers of intuition."*

How did your awareness affect your communication today? What was your first impression about something today, and was it right?

------------------------------------------------------------------------
------------------------------------------------------------------------
------------------------------------------------------------------------
------------------------------------------------------------------------
------------------------------------------------------------------------
------------------------------------------------------------------------
------------------------------------------------------------------------

**Day 20**

Morning:

*"Awareness amplifies joy and gratitude."*

What were your first thoughts when you opened your eyes? How does your body feel this morning? What emotions are present as you start your day? What are you most grateful for as you begin this day?

---
---
---
---
---
---

Evening:

*"Synchronicity is an ever-present reality for those who have eyes to see."* – Carl Jung

What sign or synchronicity did you notice today? What brought you the most joy today?

---
---
---
---
---
---
---

**Day 21**

Morning:

*"Mindfulness is the practice; awareness is the result."*

What were your first thoughts when you opened your eyes? How does your body feel this morning? What emotions are present as you start your day? What are you most grateful for as you begin this day?

------------------------------------------------------------
------------------------------------------------------------
------------------------------------------------------------
------------------------------------------------------------
------------------------------------------------------------
------------------------------------------------------------

Evening:

*"No is a complete sentence, especially when it's guided by your knowing."*

How did you practice mindfulness in your activities today? What did your intuition help you avoid or say no to today?

------------------------------------------------------------
------------------------------------------------------------
------------------------------------------------------------
------------------------------------------------------------
------------------------------------------------------------
------------------------------------------------------------
------------------------------------------------------------
------------------------------------------------------------

**Day 22**

Morning:

*"The more aware you are, the richer your experience of life becomes."*

What were your first thoughts when you opened your eyes? How does your body feel this morning? What emotions are present as you start your day? What are you most grateful for as you begin this day?

------------------------------------------------------------------------
------------------------------------------------------------------------
------------------------------------------------------------------------
------------------------------------------------------------------------
------------------------------------------------------------------------
------------------------------------------------------------------------

Evening:

*"Intuition builds bridges between people and truth."*

What new awareness did you gain about your surroundings today? How did your inner knowing guide a conversation or relationship today?

------------------------------------------------------------------------
------------------------------------------------------------------------
------------------------------------------------------------------------
------------------------------------------------------------------------
------------------------------------------------------------------------
------------------------------------------------------------------------
------------------------------------------------------------------------

**Day 23**

Morning:

*"Awareness opens the door to new perspectives."*

What were your first thoughts when you opened your eyes? How does your body feel this morning? What emotions are present as you start your day? What are you most grateful for as you begin this day?

------------------------------------------------------------
------------------------------------------------------------
------------------------------------------------------------
------------------------------------------------------------
------------------------------------------------------------
------------------------------------------------------------

Evening:

*"Alignment doesn't need proof — it just feels right."*

Did you notice any shifts in your perspective today? What decision felt aligned without needing explanation?

------------------------------------------------------------
------------------------------------------------------------
------------------------------------------------------------
------------------------------------------------------------
------------------------------------------------------------
------------------------------------------------------------
------------------------------------------------------------

## Day 24

Morning:

*"Awareness of the body is the first step to self-care."*

What were your first thoughts when you opened your eyes? How does your body feel this morning? What emotions are present as you start your day? What are you most grateful for as you begin this day?

------------------------------------------------------------
------------------------------------------------------------
------------------------------------------------------------
------------------------------------------------------------
------------------------------------------------------------
------------------------------------------------------------

Evening:

*"Peace is the presence of truth."*

How did you honour your body's needs today? What intuitive action today brought you peace?

------------------------------------------------------------
------------------------------------------------------------
------------------------------------------------------------
------------------------------------------------------------
------------------------------------------------------------
------------------------------------------------------------
------------------------------------------------------------
------------------------------------------------------------

**Day 25**

Morning:

*"Emotional awareness is the foundation of emotional intelligence."*

What were your first thoughts when you opened your eyes? How does your body feel this morning? What emotions are present as you start your day? What are you most grateful for as you begin this day?

---------------------------------------------------------------
---------------------------------------------------------------
---------------------------------------------------------------
---------------------------------------------------------------
---------------------------------------------------------------
---------------------------------------------------------------

Evening:

*"Hindsight often confirms intuition's accuracy."*

What emotions were most present for you today, and how did you handle them? If you had followed your first instinct all day, how would your day have looked different?

---------------------------------------------------------------
---------------------------------------------------------------
---------------------------------------------------------------
---------------------------------------------------------------
---------------------------------------------------------------
---------------------------------------------------------------

**Day 26**

Morning:

*"Awareness is the light that guides your spiritual journey."*
What were your first thoughts when you opened your eyes? How does your body feel this morning? What emotions are present as you start your day? What are you most grateful for as you begin this day?

------------------------------------------------------------------------
------------------------------------------------------------------------
------------------------------------------------------------------------
------------------------------------------------------------------------
------------------------------------------------------------------------
------------------------------------------------------------------------

Evening:

*"Coming home to yourself is where intuition lives."*

How did you nurture your spirit today? How did you reconnect with yourself today?

------------------------------------------------------------------------
------------------------------------------------------------------------
------------------------------------------------------------------------
------------------------------------------------------------------------
------------------------------------------------------------------------
------------------------------------------------------------------------
------------------------------------------------------------------------
------------------------------------------------------------------------

**Day 27**

Morning:

*"Awareness allows you to release what no longer serves you."*

What were your first thoughts when you opened your eyes? How does your body feel this morning? What emotions are present as you start your day? What are you most grateful for as you begin this day?

----------------------------------------------------------------
----------------------------------------------------------------
----------------------------------------------------------------
----------------------------------------------------------------
----------------------------------------------------------------
----------------------------------------------------------------

Evening:

*"Stillness is the cradle of intuition."*

What did you let go of today to make space for something new? What moment of stillness revealed something unexpected?

----------------------------------------------------------------
----------------------------------------------------------------
----------------------------------------------------------------
----------------------------------------------------------------
----------------------------------------------------------------
----------------------------------------------------------------
----------------------------------------------------------------

**Day 28**

Morning:

*"Gratitude deepens awareness and connects you to the present moment."*

What were your first thoughts when you opened your eyes? How does your body feel this morning? What emotions are present as you start your day? What are you most grateful for as you begin this day?

------------------------------------------------------------
------------------------------------------------------------
------------------------------------------------------------
------------------------------------------------------------
------------------------------------------------------------
------------------------------------------------------------

Evening:

*"Trust grows where attention flows."*

How did you practice gratitude today? What are you beginning to trust more deeply about your own inner voice?

------------------------------------------------------------
------------------------------------------------------------
------------------------------------------------------------
------------------------------------------------------------
------------------------------------------------------------
------------------------------------------------------------
------------------------------------------------------------

## Day 29

Morning:

*"Awareness is a journey, not a destination."*

What were your first thoughts when you opened your eyes? How does your body feel this morning? What emotions are present as you start your day? What are you most grateful for as you begin this day?

------------------------------------------------------------
------------------------------------------------------------
------------------------------------------------------------
------------------------------------------------------------
------------------------------------------------------------
------------------------------------------------------------

Evening:

*"Your intuition will call out what no longer belongs."*

How did your awareness evolve over the course of the day? What old story did your intuition challenge or rewrite today?

------------------------------------------------------------
------------------------------------------------------------
------------------------------------------------------------
------------------------------------------------------------
------------------------------------------------------------
------------------------------------------------------------
------------------------------------------------------------

**Day 30**

Morning:

*"Awareness is the beginning of change, and change is the beginning of growth"*

What were your first thoughts when you opened your eyes? How does your body feel this morning? What emotions are present as you start your day? What are you most grateful for as you begin this day?

------------------------------------------------------------------------
------------------------------------------------------------------------
------------------------------------------------------------------------
------------------------------------------------------------------------
------------------------------------------------------------------------
------------------------------------------------------------------------

Evening:

*"The more you trust it, the louder it becomes."*

What is the biggest shift in awareness you've experienced this month? Looking back, what has shifted in your relationship with intuition this month?

------------------------------------------------------------------------
------------------------------------------------------------------------
------------------------------------------------------------------------
------------------------------------------------------------------------
------------------------------------------------------------------------
------------------------------------------------------------------------

## NOTE FROM THE AUTHOR

Over the 3 decades of doing my own personal inner work and over a decade of working with my clients the content in this book has served me and my clients well.

As I was editing the manuscript for Spiritual A.I., and I read it over and over again, I realised how much value is in here, and I want to invite you to read and re-read this book over and over again. It will help you when you hit the next hurdle or the next relationship, or even with your next client. Don't just read it once and say, "I got it", because the truth is, I still don't "got it". This book will support us all, including me, to get a handle on life. I'm looking forward to having my book by my side to read it again and again, because even I can learn from this.

**Read it...**
**Study it...**
**Buy and Share a copy with a friend...**

**This is how we change the world!**

## ABOUT THE AUTHOR

Leonie Du Toit is a transformational coach, spiritual teacher, and intuitive healer who helps people reconnect with the intelligence that lives within them, their awareness and intuition. With a background in healing arts and a lifelong gift for seeing beneath the surface, Leonie supports others in awakening their soul's potential and living with greater clarity, ease, and purpose.

She is the founder of *Spiritual AI*, a movement dedicated to bringing awareness and intuition back to the forefront of personal growth and spiritual development. Through her teachings, private sessions, podcast, and writing, Leonie reminds us that real transformation doesn't come from outside of us. It begins when we pause, pay attention, and trust what we already know deep within.

Known for her grounded wisdom, compassionate honesty, and gift for seeing patterns others miss, Leonie has guided thousands of clients to breakthrough moments, often with a single powerful insight.

She lives in Perth, Western Australia, where she continues to create, teach, and walk her talk, one intuitive step at a time.

# NOTES

# NOTES

# NOTES

www.ingramcontent.com/pod-product-compliance
Lightning Source LLC
Chambersburg PA
CBHW032019290426
44109CB00013B/722